Charles M. (Charles Maus) Taylor

Vacation Days in Hawaii and Japan

Charles M. (Charles Maus) Taylor

Vacation Days in Hawaii and Japan

ISBN/EAN: 9783337171018

Printed in Europe, USA, Canada, Australia, Japan

Cover: Foto ©Andreas Hilbeck / pixelio.de

More available books at **www.hansebooks.com**

VACATION DAYS

IN

HAWAII AND JAPAN

BY

CHARLES M. TAYLOR, Jr.

WITH OVER ONE HUNDRED ILLUSTRATIONS

PHILADELPHIA
GEORGE W. JACOBS & CO.
1898

PREFACE.

This journal is the outline of a three months' tour in the Hawaiian Islands and Japan, supplemented by camera and sketch book, by means of which I have attempted to give some idea of the principal features of these countries, whose mountains and valleys, temples and images, castles and palaces excite our admiration or wonder at every turn. In the journey through Japan, I lead the reader by no beaten tracks, but, after visiting the most important cities, penetrate far into the heart of the country, and to districts hitherto untraveled by English-speaking people, where we have a passing glimpse of the native in his primitive mode of living, unaffected by the progress of modern civilization, and the opening of the ports to the outside world.

I am indebted to my little red-backed guide book (Murray's *Handbook of Japan*) for information on many points connected with this trip, also for historical and legendary accounts of various gods, palaces, and temples.

To every traveler in a strange land is given an individual experience, which, joined to the impressions of other travelers, helps to make a true picture of that country—and so I add my mite to the many volumes already written, feeling that much still remains unsaid regarding the customs, habits, manners, temperaments, and traditions of these most interesting people.

PHILADELPHIA,   C. M. T., JR.
   July 1, 1898.

CONTENTS.

OFF FOR THE PACIFIC COAST.

Southern scenes—Fellow-passengers—Difference in time—The Negro—Louisiana farms—At the stations—Negro cars and waiting rooms—Pecos River Bridge—Stein's Pass—Mirage—Bandits' Blunder—Chochise Mountain—Los Angeles—Pasadena, ... 15

SOME SIGHTS IN NORTHERN CALIFORNIA.

San Francisco—Places of interest—Chinatown—A prize fight—San José—Mt. Hamilton—The Lick Observatory—Santa Cruz—The " Big Trees "—Monterey and the Del Monte Hotel—The Seventeen mile Drive—Chinese fishermen—On the " Australia," 24

HONOLULU AND THE NATIVES.

The voyage—Haleakala—The leper colony—The captain's dinner—Koko Head—The harbor of Honolulu—My little pistol—A Hawaiian breakfast—Poi—Statistics—Waikiki Beach—Sharks—Surf boating—Gathering sea moss—Shopping in Honolulu—A Japanese tailor—The fish market—Cricket grounds—A " Hula Hula " dance, . . 49

PLANTATIONS AND MOUNTAINS.

Second-class cars—Native smokers—Rice plantation—Fields of sugar cane—Crushing the cane—Planting cane—

Lunch in a cocoanut grove—Pearl City and harbor—
Pineapple farm—Chinese theatres—Strangers in Honolulu—Climate—The departure of the "Australia"—To the Pali—On the summit—Ladies and the Pali—Punchbowl—Photographing the natives—Poi dog—Crab fishing, ... 71

THE HOUSE OF EVERLASTING FIRE.

Off for Hilo—Old Neptune's frolics—Views en voyage—Lanai Landing cargo—Temple of Haen—Niulii—Mountain waterfalls—Loupahoehoe—Hilo—Unpleasant bedfellows—Drive to the crater—Flume bridges—Native jungles—Japanese moving—Halfway house—Volcano hotel—The crater of Halemaumau—Kilauea—Mauna Kea—Walk to the crater—Lava formations—The House of Everlasting Fire—Candle tree—Bird's nest fern—Return to Hilo—An American circus—Cocoanut Island—Kanaka church—Native bathers—Back to Honolulu, 90

FIRST IMPRESSIONS OF JAPAN.

Departure from Honolulu—The steamship "China"—Steerage passengers—Punkahas—A morning swim—Birds' Island—Collecting fares—Chinese gamblers—Letters of introduction—Chopsticks—Yokohama harbor—Chinese merchants—Japanese guide—Streets of Yokohama—Japanese theatre—The shampooer—A Jinrikisha ride—Japanese funeral—Mississippi Bay—Negishi—Tea house of Tsukimikan, ... 113

JINRIKISHA RIDES AND NOVEL EXPERIENCES.

A Japanese afternoon tea—Shoes in Japan—Yamashita—At Mrs. Shimasaki's—The great tattooer—Seeing the "Elephant"—Wooden tickets—Maganechio—The Demi-monde—An earthquake—Sitting for our pictures—Along the canal, ... 137

KAMAKURA AND ENOSHIMA.

Kamakura—The Icho tree—Ud-di-jin and Sa di-jin—Temple of Hachiman—Onna Ishi and Otoko Ishi—Lotus Pond—Daibutsu—Temple of Kwannon—Katase—Food in Japan Enoshima—At Kinkiro Inn—Mountain cave—Goddess of Luck—Diver—Japanese money—Statistics, ... 156

TOKYO AND THE TEMPLES OF NIKKO.

Off for Tokyo—City walls—Imperial passport—Atago yama—En route for Nikko—Cryptomerias—Reiheishi Kaido—Nikko—Temples and temples—Photographs—The Great Gate—"Sleeping Cat"—Koshin—Wind and thunder devils—Sacred stable—Red Bridge—Inari, Goddess of Rice—Suminohi—Nantai zan—Daiya gawa—Images of Amida—Temple of Jokoji—God of Children—To Ashio—Dainichi-do—Snake Garden—Pilgrims—Buddhist and Shintoist—Chuzenji—Hannya and Hodo—The young prince—Kegon no taki, ... 171

IN THE HEART OF JAPAN.

A journey to the interior—Outfit—At the station—Country people—Omiya—In a second class car—Silk-growing district—Annaka—Asama yama—Iwafune-san—Miyozi san—Yokogawa—Usui Pass—Tunnels—Karuizawa—Making a bed—A bath—Iwamurata—Chikuma-gawa—Nagano—Zenkoji—Inarimura-Shimohigano—Bowing—Tanbajegma—Saigawa—Japanese Artists—A Feast—Presents—Silk-weaving mill—Night watchmen, ... 199

ON THE ROAD, AKAKURA, NAOETSU, NIIGATA.

Akakura—Hot Springs—Eating with chopsticks—A warm bath—Blackened teeth—Naoetsu—Equalization of labor—Umbrellas—Katamachi—The new railroad—Aomigawa Kashiwazaki—An inn receipt—Souvenirs—Jinrikisha rates—"Corner" in jinrikishas—Tashiro—Miyamoto—Yoita—Floods and freshets—Prayers for clear weather—Japanese steamer, ... 224

MOUNTAIN ROADS, JINRIKISHA MEN AND RAIN.

On a Japanese steamer—Aground—Niigata—Change of route—Photographing the tea girls—Kameda—A universal Panacea—Bad roads—Jinrikisha men on a strike—Tobacco fields—Yasuda—Tiffin—A curious crowd—Komatsu—Deep Gully—Agano-gawa—Dangerous road—Kuroiwa Pass—Mountain echo—Overturned jinrikisha—Tsugawa—Pipes at night—Japanese toothbrushes—Spectacles—Too much rain—Wax tree—Cedars and cryptomerias—Torii Pass—Worse and worse—Nozawa—Wakamatsu—Tabanematsu tunnel—Bridge of boats—Crossing the bridge—Bange, ... 243

FROM BANGE TO SENDAI.

Definition of a "Gentleman"—School children—Freshet—Crossing the Okawa—Carrying bundles—Wakamatsu—Japanese doorways—More shrines—Takinozawa Pass and mountain—Kutsukake—Lake Inawashiro—More rain—Yamagata—The anti-express—Nakayama Pass—Freshets again—Motomiya—Curious people—Japanese versus American customs, ... 263

FLOOD AND FRESHET.

Sendai—An "American" room—A terrible night—Bridges swept away—We abandon the northern trip—Yaita—Rivers still rising—Impassable roads—A long wet walk—Jinrikishas at last—Crowded inns—A hopeless prospect—Disease among the natives—Crossing the Kinugawa—In the rapids—Coolie back—The Furussata—Ravages of the storm—Holding the train—En route for Nikko, . . 280

TOKYO AND A CIRCULAR TOUR.

We leave Nikko—Tokyo by night—Novel sights—Fencing school—Asakusa Park—Shiba temple—Cherry banks of Koganei—Master wrestler—Carrying a god—The Tokaido—Valley of the Sakawa gawa—Gotemba—Fujiyama—Image of Kwannon—Nagoya—Shinachu hotel—Many merchants—Great earthquake of 1891—Husking rice boats—Cormorant fishing—Ibuki-yama—Lake Biwa—Vestiges of the storm, ... 294

THE CAPITAL OF FORMER DAYS.

A steamer on Lake Biwa—Kyoto—Shops—Queer combinations—The Daibutsu—Great bells of Japan—Punishing children—Burning the body—Advertisements of medicines—Servants of the gods—Supplicating the gods—Selling children—Tsumiya, Nakagawa Tokumon—Kiyomizu temple—Junk trees—Tea culture—Kinkakuji—Chion-in—The 33,333 images of Kwannon—Temple of Inari, . . 315

KOBE, OSAKA, AND NARA.

A Geisha dance—Losses by flood—On to Kobe—Nunobiki waterfalls—Iwamoto, the bamboo worker—Osaka—Satsuma ware—A wrestling match—Cotton fields—The first-class compartment—Nara—Avenue of lanterns—Tame deer—Temple of Kasuga no Miya—Daibutsu—Nara ningyo — Return to Kyoto — Sobei-Kinkozan — Young ladies' school—Kyoto castle—Imperial palace, . 335

LAST DAYS IN JAPAN.

Miyanoshita—An odd shampooer—Fujiya hotel—Bamboo canes and American climate—Hot Springs—An American breakfast—Dogashima—Yumoto—Yokohama—Farewell to Japan—On board the "Coptic"—At sea—The 180th meridian—Died at sea—First sight of land—Cricket—A candy pull—Honolulu—Soo Coolies—Leaving Honolulu—Betting on the pilot—San Francisco—Snowstorm—Summit Station—The "Rockies"—Chicago —Philadelphia, ... 350

VACATION DAYS IN HAWAII AND JAPAN.

OFF FOR THE PACIFIC COAST.

"AND he who's doomed o'er waves to roam,
Or wander on a foreign strand,
Will sigh whene'r he thinks of home
And better love his native land."
—*Leggett.*

Southern scenes — Fellow passengers — Difference in time — The Negro—Louisiana farms—At the stations—Negro cars and waiting rooms—Pecos River Bridge—Stein's Pass—Mirage —Bandits' Blunder —Chochise Mountain—Los Angeles—Pasadena.

WE leave Philadelphia, May 25th, 1896, by the Piedmont Air Line, en route for Los Angeles, via New Orleans. The heat is intense, and we find that there are drawbacks to even the most perfect conditions of railway travel in such weather.

The country is flat, and there is little to interest one in the typical Southern villages and small towns that glide by in rapid succession. Here and there wooden shanties peep out from the shade of dense thickets, with little pickaninnies rolling in the doorways, while groups of colored children, clad in blue homespun, with bare arms and legs, basking in the sun, stare at us wonderingly as we fly by. The sun is so hot! Are they trying to bleach themselves, I query, into a closer resemblance to their white brothers and sisters?

The road, on either side, is bordered by miles upon miles of reddish brown soil, more especially in Georgia and the Carolinas. I am told that it is rich and productive, affording abundant opportunities for cotton, tobacco, and sugar-cane planting. As time passes I become acquainted with some of my fellow-passengers. One is an Englishman, returning from a trip to "dear old England," another a Frenchman, also homeward bound after a visit to his native country. As I have traveled in both countries, we have many interesting conversations. On arriving at New Orleans, both cordially invite me to visit their homes, assuring me that it will give them much pleasure to show me the many places of interest in and around the city. I decline their hospitality reluctantly, as I am hastening on to the Pacific coast. A young lieutenant in our regular army, stationed in Arizona, entertains us with stories of camp life and adventures with the Indians.

A welcome shower has just fallen, the air is fresh and pure, and we begin to feel like new beings. We are making good time over a smooth, well-ballasted road, with little or no jolting. The ever-attentive porter has informed me that I will find it "red hot" crossing Texas; he is visibly relieved when I tell him that a reduction of fifteen or twenty pounds in weight will not leave me a skeleton. The usual venders of newspapers, magazines, novels, and gumdrops pass through the car at regular intervals.

We set back our watches an hour at Atlanta, Ga., an hour more at El Paso, Texas, and still another hour when we reach California. These changes represent Eastern, Middle, and Pacific time; thus "slow old Philadelphia," in at least one portion of the globe, may be said to beat her usual record.

The scenery throughout Louisiana is picturesque. On every side may be seen enchanting woodland and water views, with vistas beyond, very tempting to an artist's eye. Many times I am filled with regret that I may not stop here with sketch-book and camera, and gather a harvest for future use. The negro plays no unimportant part in this panorama; here he may be said to live his natural life—a life of poverty, judging by the cabins in sight; yet I am told that colored labor is employed here at wages averaging at from fifteen to eighteen dollars a month, and during the two months of cane cutting at from one dollar to a dollar and twenty-five cents a day. They are, however, a happy and jolly race, though careless and improvident, some of them growing to an enormous size, as I perceive in the towns and at the stations, where they are always in evidence, lounging in the sunshine.

The soil in this State produces grass, cotton, and grain equally well; in many fields corn may be seen ranging from six to eight feet "long," as the Japanese would say. For miles we are surrounded by these cornfields with scarcely a break; at intervals a cotton field appears, but corn predominates. After leaving Bouef, we see also the sugar cane, and learn that we are in one of the richest belts in the country for the growth of this product. The farms of this section are well kept and prosperous, but the houses are poor and neglected. Little or no live stock is raised, which is strange, as the sugar cane which is left to waste, after being cut and stripped, could be used profitably as food for cattle.

As there is only one "through" westward bound train from New Orleans, there is much excitement when it arrives at the various stations; the whole village turns out in its best array. The cowboy, in his red flannel shirt, trousers tucked in his top-boots of raw hide, his sombrero shifted to one side, and pistol in belt, is conspicuously picturesque.

The train is quickly surrounded by eager inquirers for mail and news, and many a heart beats with unexpected joy or sadness as it speeds on its way again.

There is a separate waiting room at these stations with its placard "For Negroes"; cars also, especially provided for negro travel, are attached to our train;

thus is the line of demarcation between the two races never allowed to fade out.

As we proceed, the character of the country changes materially; the soil is poorer, the crops noticeably less. Now a field of cane or cotton is rarely seen; only poor pasture land, which grows ever more barren and sandy.

Jacksonville is our last station in the State of Louisiana; it is two hundred and forty-six miles west of New Orleans. We have covered this distance in ten hours.

Six miles east of Orange we enter the State of Texas.

We have just left San Antonio, Texas, five hundred and seventy-one miles west of New Orleans. We are much entertained by observing the various types of Western life at the stations, and the old-fashioned turnouts, each with its "bony broncho" attached. Very pathetic is the appearance of some of these dwellers in the wilderness; no jingle of chains, no gold or silver mounted harness is here, or fashionable pose, or "latest" costume.

On either side of us are large tracts covered with natural grass and a bush named mesquite, which grows from a height of from two to ten feet. This bush affords both shade and food for cattle, producing a berry similar to the locust; the cattle like it, and it is fattening.

I enjoy greatly the conversation of the owner of a large ranch, who has had much experience in gold-mining and cattle-raising. He is quite social, and his tales of the dangers and hardships of early Western life would fill a volume. Although the railroad passes through large cattle ranches, we are unlikely to see any cattle, as the herds generally seek quarters as far as possible from signs of civilization.

An abundance of rice of excellent quality is raised here.

The day is oppressively hot; great clouds of dust are driven through the car windows, and the thermometer overhead in the shade registers 100° at 4.30 P. M.

We are approaching Comstock Station, one thousand five hundred and fifty-six feet above the level of the sea, and will soon cross the famous Pecos River Bridge, the second bridge in the world in height. It spans the Pecos River in Texas, and is one of the finest illustrations of modern skill.

The enormous structure rises to a height of three hundred and twenty-eight feet, and measures two thousand one hundred and eighty-four feet from end to end. Its greatest breadth, in the centre, is eight hundred feet. I have taken several photographs of this marvel of man's ingenuity. The train moves over it very slowly, as there is but a single track, with a footpath on either side.

There is little to interest one in to-day's travel; nothing but barren wastes and deserts; sand—sand—sand everywhere.

It is 7.30 P. M., the sun is shining vigorously, and although our altitude is two thousand one hundred and six feet, the temperature in our car is ninety-eight degrees.

The passengers are social and agreeable, and time passes pleasantly in conversation, games, and occasional songs.

Last night, at twenty minutes past one, we passed over the highest point on the route, an elevation of five thousand and eighty-two feet.

The heat is still intense, registering one hundred and four degrees in the shade. This, combined with the dust that drifts continually through the car, gives us all the appearance of actors in a minstrel show.

As we approach the celebrated Stein's Pass we have an interesting experience; from the car platform may be seen one of the finest mirages that it is possible to witness. It is a picture of the ocean, with the waves rolling and dashing on the sandy beach. We have several of these optical illusions, of various characters. Sometimes the water is blue, sometimes green or yellow, as the rays of the sun happen to strike it. Then, as if by magic, we have a heavy downpour of real water, a rare event here in the desert, and more than acceptable.

Several months ago an overland west-bound passenger train was "held up" at this pass by bandits, who side-tracked one of the cars, supposed to carry coin, and allowed the others to proceed. The robbers blew open the iron safe, only to discover that they had chosen the wrong car; the treasure sped safely on to its destination.

Along the mountain-side can be seen the old overland wagon trail, used before the great iron belt connected the West with the East. On the left is Chochise Mountain. Looking at its topmost peak, one may easily discern the perfect profile of a human face; the head appears to rest upon the summit, and look heavenward, as though satisfied to gaze thus forever. Tradition says that the chief of the Chochise tribe is buried there, and the profile is an eternal and lofty monument to the memory of a noble warrior.

I could write indefinitely of the legends and strange stories thus spun off by the hour, and listened to by the passengers with unwearying interest. The time passes rapidly, and almost before we are aware of it we are in the city of Los Angeles.

With only a passing glimpse of the chief city of Southern California, I hasten away from its beautiful gardens, its palms and cypress groves, its streets bordered with graceful pepper and stately eucalyptus trees, and, passing the many vineyards outside the city, speed on to Pasadena, which is my first stopping-place.

Even here, although the wild and picturesque region beyond the city limits, the charming drives and fragrant orange groves tempt one to linger, we indulge in a breathing spell of a few days only, making several short trips in the neighborhood, and are again en route, this time for San Francisco.

SOME SIGHTS IN NORTHERN CALIFORNIA.

San Francisco--Places of interest—Chinatown—Prize fight—San José — Mt. Hamilton — The Lick Observatory — Santa Cruz —" Big Trees "—Monterey and the Del Monte Hotel—Seventeen-mile Drive —Chinese fishermen—On the " Australia."

WE are in San Francisco. How odd and interesting the city appears—built on the hills, with the cable cars running up and down its steep streets that remind one of toboggan slides!

There are many interesting places to visit in and around the city—Sutro's Garden; Cliff House, with the Seal Rocks in full view from its piazza; the Presidio; Golden Gate Park; the shipyards; markets, where only one can realize the profusion and perfection of California fruits.

A visit to Chinatown is not the least of our curious experiences. It is hardly necessary to say that we make our arrangements to see the Celestial shopkeepers at night.

Chinatown has a population of twenty-five thousand souls, of whom six hundred are women, and of these, at least five hundred of more than doubtful morals. We start out one evening with a good guide, who leads us first to the most noted Joss House in "'Frisco." We ascend two flights of stairs, and pass through a high and elaborately-carved doorway, where we are met by an important Chinese official, the sole medium of communication with the great god's eyes and ears. Proceeding to the main altar, we behold the " god of

CALIFORNIA STREET, FROM NOB HILL.

all gods " in his temple. He is of homely appearance, painted red, and decked with gold and silver, spears, bows and arrows, and surrounded by emblems of peace as well as implements of war. In his left hand are lighted candles of wax, and many kinds of incense fill the air with spicy odors. A small gold-plated wooden horse stands at the god's right hand; upon it he is supposed to take his daily rides. Fresh tea is constantly placed before the idol, that his godliness may drink when he is thirsty. The guide asks if we wish special offerings made to the god for our safe journey and for protection during our absence from home. Upon our signs of assent the old priest performs a ceremony with an air of great satisfaction. After much praying, with intervals of silence, before the wooden god, we are informed that a "special record" has been made, and that all things will favor our undertaking. The room is highly ornamented with wood-carvings and silken draperies, and other characteristic decorations. Before leaving we make a small offering to the priest in return for his good offices in our behalf.

We are conducted next to a drug store, in which we find a collection of herbs supposed to cure all diseases. The walls are lined with innumerable drawers, each bearing a label in Chinese script. They are opened for our edification, and a medley of dried snakes, toads, locusts, frogs, roaches, and the like meets our eyes. These inviting specimens are prescribed for and administered to patients for their various ailments. We are not informed how many die in consequence.

Our next visit is to a gambling den. Gambling is permitted in this quarter by the authorities. I believe that "fan-tan" is the only game prohibited by law. Miserable-looking creatures surround the tables here, and venture small amounts with an eagerness worthy of a better cause. This is the nightly experience of these poor souls, who are ignorant of anything beyond a present existence.

Here is a pawnbroker's shop, with many strange things on its walls and shelves; besides old watches and jewelry, here are objects whose use no human being could explain. These articles have been left here by poor wretches for the loan of a few nickels. The owner of the shop is fat and jolly looking; whoever loses in these transactions, it is quite evident that he is not the sufferer.

We now enter a goldsmith's place, where rings, breastpins, cuff-buttons, and other articles of jewelry are manufactured. If one wishes a piece made after a particular pattern he orders it, the price is fixed, and the article is delivered when finished. Should the purchaser grow weary of his bargain he may return it to the manufacturer, who will allow him full value for the gold, retaining only the price of his time and labor.

Crossing the street, we find ourselves in the finest café, the Delmonico of Chinatown. We ascend to the second floor, which is the aristocratic portion of the building, and enter a spacious apartment, whose walls are profusely decorated with carved paneling. Fancy chairs and capacious tables are placed about the room. We seat ourselves at one of the tables, and are served by a Chinese waiter with an assortment of dainty dishes, but we do not know what we are eating; the food may be a concoction of choice morsels of rat, cat, or dog, or a combination of all three. Only the better class of Chinamen use this room; others are served on the first floor.

I have long wished to see a genuine Chinese opium den, and now my wish is gratified; we are led by our guide to a dark, musty place containing many wooden beds, upon which are stretched out or huddled together the emaciated forms of the slaves of this vile habit. For twenty-five cents one can obtain fifteen cents worth of opium and lodging in one of these dens to sleep off the effect of the drug.

The opium habit is so general in this section that merchants, druggists, and other tradesmen have beds and opium pipes in the corners of their stores and offices. It is not uncommon, on the occasion of a friendly visit, for the host to ask his guest to take a pipe of opium and remain over night. We see an instance of this kind in the rooms of a Chinaman and his wife; two friends have come to visit them, and here they lie, all four completely stupefied, and under the influence of the drug till morning.

Through special courtesy shown to our guide we are permitted to enter a Chinese theatre by the back door, thus obtaining a sight of the green room and the actors' quarters. In the former, the actors, who are all men, are painting their faces and dressing themselves in such hideous effects as to suggest a nightmare to my unaccustomed American sensibilities. The rooms in which the actors live, eat, and sleep are indescribably loathsome, situated far underground, beneath the theatre, and of the smallest dimensions—four feet by six by five. They are filthy and malodorous.

Now we are directly back of the scenes. What a medley of queer things and people! Painted and masked faces peer at us from unrecognizable objects; soldiers, native and other characters stand out from a jumble of incongruous surroundings—a picture of Hades and its inhabitants.

We pass on to the stage, where chairs have been placed for us. The audience, composed of Chinese men and women, are in the pit and gallery. Such dancing, shouting, and jumping, such grotesque acting could not be surpassed by a band of Zulu warriors. In an hour we have enough of this performance, and leave the theatre, the deafening noise of the cymbals and brass drums ringing in our ears long afterward. I suppose the audience numbered about two hundred.

How delightful to be out in the fresh air again after

the heavy atmosphere and the vile smoke from the pipes in the theatre! But we congratulate ourselves too soon. As we enter a neighboring grocery store a stronger and more objectionable odor greets our olfactories. You could never guess what this store sells to the people of Chinatown. Somewhat costly articles,

STREET SCENE IN CHINATOWN, CAL.

too! Hens' eggs imbedded in mud, and really imported from China.

Think of the delicious soup made from them! We are assured that this soup, made of eggs three or four months old, is a great delicacy. Here are also salt fish, sharks' fins, dried oysters, seaweed, and various vegetables, all in a state of decomposition and exhaling odors anything but pleasant. The jars of preserves, jams, pickles, and spices are delusions and snares, treacherous to the most confiding epicure. We are told that these grocers import all their goods from China.

The Chinese, both at home and abroad, are clannish, always giving the preference to home productions.

Chinese workmen, such as shoemakers, clothiers, etc., receive from a dollar to a dollar and twenty-five cents a day, and work from 8 A. M. till 9 P. M.; some of them are employed until eleven o'clock at night.

After three hours spent among their haunts we leave the Chinamen, hoping that some day a liberal contribution will be made to send the hard-working missionary into their midst, to try at least to reform these forlorn and deluded creatures, who bear so little resemblance to God's handiwork.

Great posters and placards on walls and fences, as well as unlimited matter in the daily papers, announce that the contest between James J. Corbett, the "Champion of the World," and Thomas Sharkey, is to take place at the Mechanics' Pavilion, San Francisco, on the 2d of June. The affair is under the auspices of the "National Athletic Club of Physical Culture, for the benefit of the Children's Hospital."

I ask how it is that prize-fighting is allowed in a well-regulated city like San Francisco, and why for the benefit of the Children's Hospital? I am told that prize-fighting is permitted by law, on condition that a certain portion of the proceeds is devoted to charity; in this case the amount set apart for the hospital is from two hundred and fifty to five hundred dollars. So the government closes its eyes to one of the most brutal entertainments of the age.

As some ten thousand or more spectators are to be present, I finally compromise with my conscience, and, yielding to my curiosity, decide to join the throng that will fill the vast pavilion to witness the match for the national belt.

Purchasing a ticket of admission for three dollars, I find myself in a good position, overlooking the great mass of men—with one exception. I perceive a young girl sitting close to the raised platform, and learn later that she is a reporter for one of the city newspapers.

Suddenly a bell rings loudly, and a man of large proportions appears upon the platform. The great throng becomes as silent as the grave. However, he announces only the lesser satellites of the ring, and two young men of light weight, slender forms, and brutal faces, step upon the stage. They seem to lack intelligence as well as refinement. Time is called, the opponents shake hands, then proceed to fight. Blow after blow is dealt; after a half-dozen rounds the referee declares the bout a "draw," and the men retire, having stirred the audience to but little excitement.

Two manly fellows follow, strong and well built, who, after the customary etiquette of the ring, enter upon an earnest and vigorous battle; in the third round one of the antagonists plants a well-directed blow upon the neck of his adversary, with such force that the man falls to the ground, and lies there stunned; at the last call he rises with great effort, only to fall back again so helplessly that he is assisted from the ring, while the victor, descending from the platform, is greeted with a tremendous uproar of applause.

All are now awaiting the champions in breathless excitement, but there is much delay, and the impatient multitude fill the air with vociferous calls and cheers; still they come not.

Finally, amid deafening applause, the great "Sharkey" ascends the platform; every time the powerful athlete bows his friends in the audience respond with rousing cheers. He moves quietly to his place in the ring and seats himself; his expression is determined and confident.

In a few moments the world-renowned champion, "James Corbett," makes his appearance. It is impossible to describe the tumult that follows. Men shout themselves hoarse; hats, canes, and papers are thrown in the air, and those whose excitement knows no bounds, jump up and down on their chairs.

At last order is restored, and the great throng hushed, yet there are still many delays and preliminaries; the details must be perfect, for the result of this fight will be carried over the wires from west to east, and to every quarter of the globe.

Everything is now ready, and amid utter silence the athletes rise and walk towards each other. They stand during a minute of intense stillness, and, looking over the crowd, the observer is impressed with the importance of the occasion.

The signal is given, and the rivals shake hands; then the battle begins; hard blows are rapidly exchanged.

The audience is silent and orderly, the only sounds heard being those made by the combatants. At the end of three minutes the bell announces a rest, and the tumult begins again. Cheers and shouts resound through the hall, now for "Corbett," now for "Sharkey."

At the tap of the bell the champions spring to their feet with the nimbleness of cats. This round is more violent than the other; another rest and a bout. When the third round is finished, the blood streaming from the face of one of the men, and the great lumps disfiguring the countenance of both, render the spectacle utterly revolting.

On the fourth and last round they fight furiously and savagely, spurred on by the large sum at stake and the fame of the championship. They are so brutal in their attacks, and rush on each other with such reckless disregard of the rules of the ring that the referee is compelled to call in the attending officers to separate them, which is not accomplished without great difficulty. The whole affair is so disgraceful that it is brought to a close by the interference of the police. The referee announces a "draw." Upon this the noise and confusion that ensue are beyond description. I doubt if it could be exceeded by the roar of Niagara. Swearing, tearing of programs, yells, smashing of chairs, shouts of "Bribery!" "A lie!" "A cheat!" mingle with groans and hisses.

It is long before the great sea of angry and disappointed people, still muttering threats and imprecations, slowly vacates the hall.

As I am the last to leave, I look around upon the confusion and wreck of chairs and benches, and realize that I have been to a prize fight, and that brutality and barbarism did not die out with the eighteenth century.

We have planned a trip to San José, the Lick Observatory, Santa Cruz, and Monterey, previous to our departure for the Hawaiian Islands and Japan.

San José is one of the loveliest of California's cities. The hotel to which we are driven is a fine building, spacious and elegant, situated in a delightful grove, with a lawn of exquisite beauty; a perfect haven of rest to the tired traveler. The rooms are comfortable, and the service that of a first-class hotel.

We have engaged seats on the stage for the drive to and from the Lick Observatory.

At 12.30 P. M., on the day following our arrival, the stage, drawn by four well-kept black horses, appears at the door of our hotel, and we take our places therein in company with others of our party; the whip is cracked, the reins tightened, and we are off on a journey of fifty-four miles.

For some distance the dust plays a prominent part with passengers as well as landscape, but there are few complaints, as this is the inevitable accompaniment of California drives, and we are all enthusiastic over the treat in store for us.

Now we ascend, now descend by a well-graded carriage road, the view growing finer as we gradually increase our altitude.

In the distance the fields of San José look like a checker-board, while the houses seem like specks on the picture.

When we have driven ten miles we stop to change horses and take some refreshment, starting again in a short time with renewed speed. The country is more and more interesting. Far off in the distance we can see Mt. Hamilton, upon whose topmost peak the Lick Observatory is situated.

It is nearly five o'clock in the afternoon; we stop at a small hotel, change horses, and partake of a substantial supper. The hotel is at the base of Mt. Hamilton, and we have still a drive of seven miles before us ere we reach our destination. With strong horses we start once more on our upward journey. The road is a marvel of modern engineering.

Higher and higher we ascend; our trusty horses never falter or stumble. These horses are used only on this winding road; thus accuracy of step and sureness of foot is secured, and there is little or no danger of accident.

What grandeur surrounds us! Far away on the right and left the tops of adjacent mountains are visible; close by us a tall pine tree shoots out from the side of the mountain, overlooking the deep cañon below; in its topmost branch an eagle, jealous of her location, has built her nest where she may rear her young undisturbed. Another turn in the road, and we are in the presence of one of Nature's grandest pictures.

From the very edge of the path we can overlook the great cañon fully three thousand feet beneath. I shudder thinking of our fate, if one of the horses should stumble, or a wheel of the coach give way! But a happier inspiration tells me that it would mean only the change from our mortal to a heavenly state.

On and on we go, till it seems that the mountain has no summit. We do not reach it until we have attained an altitude of four thousand four hundred and forty-four feet. Meanwhile the road has become quite narrow—only wide enough for one vehicle.

We are now so high that we have a magnificent view of the surrounding country; the finest prospect in this region, and one which is considered the chief attraction of the drive.

At last we have reached the summit, having made three hundred and forty-seven turns in the road from the base of the mountain, a distance, as I have said, of seven miles.

We leave the stage with aching joints, and enter the great observatory, whose fame is so world-wide that it is unnecessary for me to give any description of it here.

As it is too early in the evening to view the planets through the wonderful telescope, we spend the intervening time on the roof of the observatory. I feel that no words of mine can adequately describe the scene before us. The setting sun casts a golden and crimson glow over the landscape; the great masses of cloud far below us seem like the boundless sea, with here and there stupendous breakers rolling and tumbling in the glory of this vivid and translucent flame. It is awe-inspiring. All about us is silent and still. I feel the omnipotence of the Divine Master! A sense of remoteness from the active bustling world overpowers one—a feeling of unreality. Resting here at this immense height, I feel

> "Like one who wraps the drapery of his couch about him
> And lies down to pleasant dreams."

Aye, wondrous visions! Shall I ever forget the spectacle!

The evening advances, and the hour is favorable. We look through the great telescope at the planets Jupiter and Saturn. Yes, we gaze through the largest telescope in the world! How great the privilege! The heavens are unveiled to us in all their glory!

One of the professors connected with the observatory gives us an interesting account of the planets now visible. We spend several hours with the professor and the wonderful glass, then start on our return down the mountain. The moon now appears in all her glory to lighten the dangerous way, and add to our confidence. Thus we, too, are favored by Divine Providence, even as the Israelites of old, while crossing the desert.

As the horses trot down the steep and winding way, it requires but little effort of the imagination to feel that we are floating or flying through the air, instead of riding in a wagon with hard, inflexible springs. Our hearts beat quickly as we approach the turns in the road, and a sense of relief follows as each one is rounded in safety.

Surely we must be near level ground now, for the trees, for the first time since we started, stretch out their long, black branches far above our heads. Yes, we have reached the plain, and here is the hotel at the foot of Mt. Hamilton.

We should thank our Creator that safety was with us; but being of earthly mold, we are more inclined to be grateful to our driver for deliverance from danger. The descents and ascents of the afternoon are gradually retraced. A dense mist surrounds us, obscuring the view, and rendering this part of the drive uninteresting.

We reach the Hotel Vendome at 1.30 A. M., and soon after retire to bed, to live over in dreamland the experience of a happy day.

We leave San José at 10.17 the following morning for Santa Cruz, the City of the Holy Cross. Upon arriving, we go directly to our hotel, which is beautifully situated, overlooking the placid bay of Monterey.

Santa Cruz is a small city of not more than seven thousand souls; its pleasures are naturally confined to sea-bathing, sailing, fishing, and last, but not least, flirting and love-making.

There are several delightful drives and walks hereabout; the most interesting are the "Cliffs" and the picturesque road along the San Lorenzo River and ravine to the " Big Trees."

A morning stroll to the " Cliffs " more than repays us. The wild, rocky coast, with the huge waves dashing constantly against it is a delight to the artist's soul.

The drive to the " Big Trees," along the bank of the San Lorenzo and through a rugged ravine, is extremely picturesque.

The grove of the " Big Trees " is about six miles from the town. Shortly after leaving the hotel we plunge abruptly into a wild forest; on every side are tall and stately redwood, pine, and poplar trees, whose great branches rise far above our heads. Some of the trees attain to a height of from one to two hundred feet, not merely one here and there among trees of smaller growth, but hundreds that are massive and lofty.

Now we ford the river, and in a few minutes reach the grove of " Big Trees."

What solemn grandeur looms up here! As we penetrate the forest we are surrounded by giants whose ages number among the thousands.

The most prominent among them are : " The Giant," measuring 60 feet in circumference and 300 feet in height; " General Fremont," 46 feet in circumference and 275 feet in height; " Jumbo," 48 feet in circumference and 270 feet in height; " General Grant," 56 feet in circumference and 300 feet in height; " Daniel Webster," 40 feet in circumference and 275 feet in height; "Y. M. C. A." group, 78 feet in circumference, 300 feet high; "Ingersoll's Cathedral," 95 feet in circumference, 300 feet high.

I could mention many more, but the above list will serve to give an idea of the forest of "Big Trees."

We remain four days in Santa Cruz, then wend our way to that most famous of all California resorts, the Del Monte Hotel at Monterey.

The hotel is only half a mile from the station, where we find a comfortable coach with four good horses waiting to take passengers thither.

Our room on the second floor is pleasantly situated, well furnished, and comfortable, with bath and all conveniences.

Having freed ourselves from the dust of travel, we roam about the extensive and beautiful grounds. The hotel stands in the centre of a tract of one hundred and forty acres of lawn and woodland. It is the largest hotel on the Pacific coast and perfect in all its appointments. It is impossible, in words, to do justice to this mass of grandeur and magnificence, one of the most beautiful spots I have ever beheld. Here are hundreds of lovely bowers, picturesque flower-beds, with every kind of blossom perfuming the air, great trees with wide-spreading branches shading velvety lawns; birds filling the air with melody, and beautiful women moving about the spacious halls and wandering among the shady groves. Music entrances the soul and ideal comfort abounds everywhere.

The scene gives one the idea of a little world, including all the treasures of the universe.

At night the gayety is at its height. The dance in the vast ball-room, where among the throng of brilliant costumes may be seen the latest creations of Worth; the billiard tables in the ladies' parlor, surrounded by expert men and women players; ten-pin alleys, conversation and card-rooms, smoking dens, the nooks on the piazzas where the electric light has no admission and the ardent lover may plead his cause before a Venus of modern fashion; all are upon a magnificent scale. The hotel is capable of accommodating a thousand guests.

Monterey is about to celebrate the semi-centennial anniversary of the settlement of California, 1846–1896. This is the 3d of July; the festivities are to be held on the 4th, 5th, 6th, and 7th of the month.

A walk to the town assures one that something unusual is going on; a busier place could hardly be found. Shopkeepers, tradesmen, and others are zealously engaged in draping bunting and mounting flags. Every inhabitant, old and young, is preparing for his or her share in the celebration. Every store and house in the place is gay with the national colors.

Monterey is a small place—so small, in fact, that I would not hesitate to call it a village, and even that on no very large scale. It was settled by Mexicans, and the houses are small and either frame or adobe; they are washed or painted white, which gives the city a clean appearance.

Many Mexicans, with their sallow faces shaded by wide-brimmed sombreros, are here, standing in groups at the street corners discussing the approaching holidays.

Saturday, July 4th.—This is the first day of the celebration. We are on hand in good season.

First on the programme is a naval manœuvre by the men-of-war at anchor in the bay, the "Philadelphia" and the monitor "Monadnock." At twelve o'clock there is a gre͞ ͞ring of cannon, witnessed by a large assembly o͞ ͞ ͞e beach and edge of the town. When the ͞ ͞ ͞ ͞ve died away the crowd moves to the ͞ ͞ ͞ accordance with the programme. Th͞ ͞ ͞ ͞ ͞ ͞ are under the management of the ͞ ͞ ͞ ͞ and Parlor, Native Daughters of the Golden West." The members of this society head the procession, the lady commander on horseback. After them come the officers and seamen of the "Philadelphia" and the "Monadnock," followed by cannon and artillery. A large float, representing the Goddess of Liberty, is received by the people with enthusiasm.

SOME SIGHTS IN NORTHERN CALIFORNIA. 45

Two hundred young girls from the neighboring colleges, dressed in the colors of the Union, march down the street, and take their places on a stand built for the occasion; when they are seated they present a true living picture of our national flag. Cheer after cheer expresses the appreciation of the populace for this novel and beautiful tableau.

When quiet is restored the bands play national airs, and appropriate and patriotic addresses are made by ladies of the society of the " Native Daughters of the Golden West."

These speeches, historical as well as patriotic, receive much applause.

Hops and dances at the hotels and public halls are announced for the evening. A large placard, placed conspicuously in the corridor of the D{ ' Monte Hotel, states that a "Grand Hop" will be gi· ere.

About nine o'clock the ball-room is ·. .l to overflowing with fashionably-dressed ladies ar ι gentlemen. A fine orchestra is awaiting the signal ∴ the master of ceremonies, light refreshments are .iced on convenient tables, and the hall is lavishly decorated with plants and flowers.

The music bursts forth, hundreds of feet glide over the polished floor, and without any effort one can imagine himself transported to fairy-land.

The music is still ringing in our ears as we enter our

room at a late hour, and with its strains ends the "Glorious Fourth," the pride and joy of every true American in the West as well as in the East.

To-day we take the seventeen-mile drive, one of the chief attractions of this place. Leaving the hotel at two o'clock in the afternoon, with a fine pair of horses, we drive through the old town of Monterey, passing the first jail, post-office and custom house built in the State. These buildings date back to about 1770 A. D. Here, too, the first American flag was raised in California.

Leaving Monterey, our road skirts the bay. Off in the distance, upon the water's edge, may be seen an old Chinese fishing settlement. The Chinamen pack their fish in salt, and ship them directly to China; as there is a heavy duty on salt, these so-called slow Chinese pack the greater part of their barrels with salt, the lesser with fish, thus evading the vigilant eyes of Uncle Sam's officials.

We drive through Pacific Grove, a religious settlement, similar to that at Ocean Grove, New Jersey.

Now leaving the bay we are on the Pacific Ocean beach. What a fine and extensive view! The great rocks jutting out of the water afford resting places for thousands of ducks, pelicans, and other wild fowl. Here and there are smaller rocks, over which the waves dash, throwing their spray high in the air. Several

SOME SIGHTS IN NORTHERN CALIFORNIA. 47

miles farther on are the Seal Rocks, and a drive of a mile or more brings us to the end of the peninsula, which is called Carmel Point. Here we rest the horses and enjoy a beautiful view of country and ocean. Cypress trees grow from crevices in the rocks at the very edge of the water.

Our drive is a circuitous one; when we reach an elevation of five hundred feet we can see the Hotel Del Monte facing us in the distance, amid its stately groves of oak and pine; a half-hour later we reach its hospitable doors once more, and looking at our watches, find that we have been absent just three hours.

To-morrow, at 8.45 in the morning, we leave this gay and interesting spot for San Francisco, going directly to the Palace Hotel, where we will remain until Saturday, July 11th, when our steamer, the "Australia," will sail for the Hawaiian Islands.

We are anxious to be off, feeling that our greatest sight-seeing will begin when we bid adieu to our dear America.

What might befall us the next few months time alone can tell. The traveler at all times takes his life in his hands; but at home, or among a strange people in foreign lands, or on the pathless sea, we trust ever in Him whose loving wisdom orders all things well.

The day of our departure from San Francisco has

arrived; the usual preparations for a long ocean voyage have been made.

At nine o'clock in the morning a carriage awaits us in the courtyard of the hotel, and, with steamer trunks, chairs, and rugs, we are driven to the Fulsom Street pier, where the "Australia" is moored. Our staterooms, comfortable and well ventilated, are on the promenade deck. At exactly ten o'clock the whistle sounds, the steamer casts off her moorings, and with the bustle and confusion of departure, "Good-bye" and "God bless you," in many keys, still ringing in our ears, we break away from the shore, and find ourselves out in the middle of the bay.

The steamer is to be our little world for the next six days. We are cut off from all communication with any human beings save those around us; dependent upon ourselves and each other. A slight feeling of sadness overcomes us, and we begin to talk of the loved ones in our far-off home.

HONOLULU AND THE NATIVES.

The voyage—Haleakala—Leper colony—Captain's dinner—Koko Head—Harbor of Honolulu—Revenue officers—Hawaiian breakfast—Poi—Statistics—Waikiki beach—Sharks—Surf boating—Gathering sea moss—Shopping in Honolulu—Japanese tailor—Fish market—Cricket grounds—"Hula Hula" dance.

WE glide swiftly and smoothly down the bay and through the Golden Gate to the sea; as soon as we meet the waters of the ocean the steamer begins to plunge from side to side; the change from the calm bay and clear sky to rough waves and fog is sudden, and not very pleasant in its effects.

One by one the passengers seek their staterooms, some from fatigue, others for reasons more apparent.

An uneventful night, with more or less rolling, carries us far out to sea; we learn in the morning that the wind has driven us fully twenty-five miles out of our course.

To-day old ocean is more placid, the air dry and pleasant. The passengers appear again on deck, and good feeling and sociability prevail. We are happy to find so many charming and congenial people on board. The captain is the jovial personage that we often read about; his good humor and kindness make sunshine wherever he is. We are fortunate enough to have seats at his left hand at table, and as there is an unusually agreeable company, meal-time is a season of bright and interesting conversation. We also have fine appetites for the good things provided by the steward, and the danger of becoming sick is more from over-eating than from over-rolling of the ship.

The days are perfect. The ocean is smooth and calm, well deserving its name; its deep purple hue spreads as far as the eye can see.

Every one on board seems well and happy; games, such as pitching quoits, sand bags and the like, fill the daylight hours, while the evenings are passed pleasantly in promenades, conversation, music, cards, and reading.

It is a beautiful night, the moon illumines sky and sea. The grandeur of the ocean, with its long regular waves broken here and there by white caps, fills me with awe. As I look upon the boundless scene, perfect above and below, my thoughts wander homeward across the distance that daily grows greater between us and our dear friends in Philadelphia. When we reach the Hawaiian Islands we will be about five thousand miles from the dearest spot on earth to us.

The thermometer to-day is eighty degrees in the shade at four o'clock in the afternoon. There is little happening worthy of note. We see our first whale, a fine large fellow, swimming leisurely along, quite near the ship, and spouting water at frequent intervals. Flying fish are seen in large numbers; sometimes we sail through a school of the pretty creatures, who flutter about us greatly frightened.

At breakfast this morning the captain informs us that we will have our first sight of land before sunset, so, after packing trunks, rugs, etc., we loiter about deck. Gazing idly over the waste of waters, and counting the gulls that continually follow the ship, I behold one of the most beautiful scenes with which an ocean voyager can be favored.

Great clouds are banked upon the left, like mountains thousands of feet high, softly tinted by the rays of the sun. At this moment the captain asks me if I can see the great Haleakala, the largest extinct crater in the world, upon the island of Maui. Yes, I see it distinctly peeping through the clouds like an enormous watch tower. Then the island of Molokai, now ten miles distant, comes into view. Apparently on the very edge of the sea rises a small hill. This is the Leper settlement. We look through the glasses, straining our eyes to catch a glimpse of the houses, but can distinguish nothing; the horizon and the sea engulf them.

What a weird and awful place to live! Before them extends the boundless ocean, and back of them rise the lofty mountains and precipices of the island. These forlorn people are thus held prisoners, access to the outside world being entirely cut off. The Hawaiian government provides for all their needs, requiring neither rent nor taxes from them, and allows all that is possible to render them comfortable and contented.

On our right, almost at the bow of the steamer, is the island of Oahu. The city of Honolulu, which is our destination, is situated upon this island. We hope to arrive about six o'clock this evening.

On the last day of an ocean voyage it is customary for the captain to give a champagne dinner to the passengers of the first class. On this occasion I am requested to be speaker. As the hour approaches, I am escorted to the promenade deck, where the company is assembled, each provided with a tin horn, pan, bucket, or other resounding instrument. We walk into the dining-room in Indian file, and then break into uproarious confusion. The noise is almost deafening. Speeches are made expressing the appreciation of all the passengers for the uniform kindness and consideration received during the voyage. The captain is quite overwhelmed by our enthusiasm.

We can now see Koko Head, a prominent rocky peak, at the extreme end of the island of Oahu. As we steam nearer, we behold a beautiful picture. The sides of the mountain are covered with lava from the extinct crater; vegetation has sprung up in the crevices, and the sun shining over all, produces a lovely effect of wonderful colors.

At the base of the mountain and along the beach are hundreds of tropical trees, such as the algeroba, the

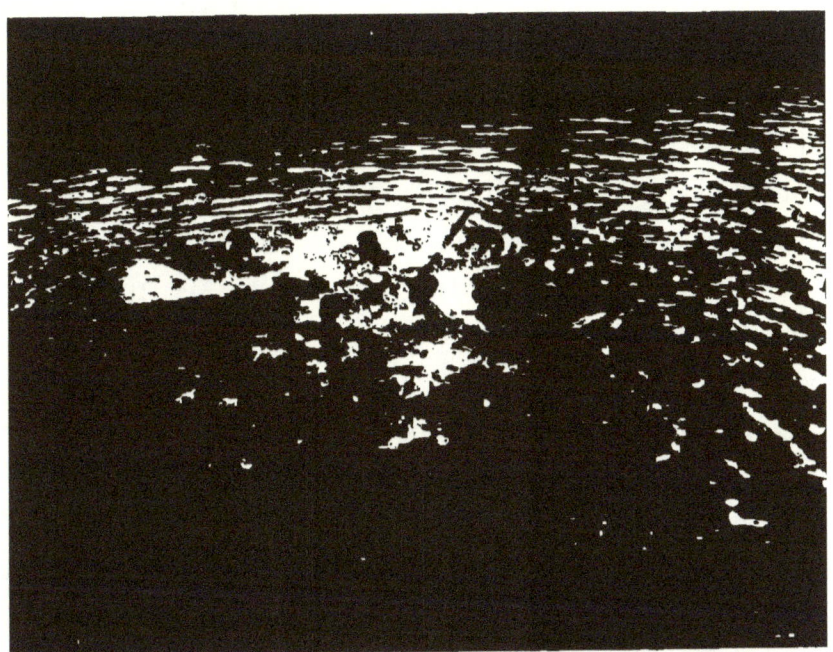

"Shouting Lustily for Nickels."

palm, cocoanut, and others of rich and luxuriant foliage. The first of these yields a bean ten to fourteen inches long, which falls when ripe, is dried and used as food for cattle.

We are now passing the Manoa Valley and Waikiki

Beach. The scenery throughout is rich in color and of uncommon beauty.

There is abundant pasturage back in the valley and upon the mountain slopes.

Looming up before us are Diamond Head and Punch Bowl, both extinct craters.

With indescribable feelings we enter the harbor of Honolulu.

Before reaching the pier we are attracted to the side of the steamer by loud calls from the native children, and, looking down into the water, see about twenty-five boys, ranging from ten to eighteen years of age, quite naked, shouting lustily to us to throw nickels to them. We are amazed to see these boys dive for the coins. They are excellent swimmers and wonderfully expert, invariably catching a piece as small as a dime before it can sink to the bottom.

An interesting native and local picture is before us. Among the large crowd assembled on the pier to receive friends and relatives from the steamer are Americans, Englishmen, Portuguese, Kanakas, Japanese, and Chinese.

The revenue officers are very strict at this port in regard to two articles—whiskey and fire-arms. As I have a little of the former and one piece of the latter some suspicion falls on me.

HONOLULU AND THE NATIVES. 55

A statement is taken of my name, age, address, and general appearance, how long I expect to remain on the islands, and my destination. All this on account of my cruel little pistol. The custom house officers inform me that if I wish to regain the weapon I must apply at the police marshal's office. I reply that I do not desire to

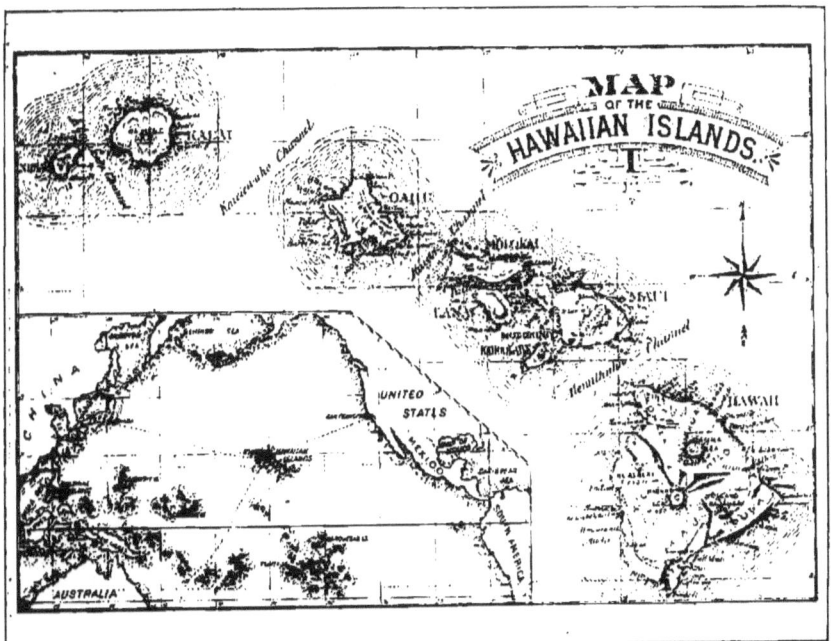

carry it, and that some of my friends who are returning to the "States" may take possession of it. This seems satisfactory. The islands are under strict military rule, and great precaution is necessary to prevent insurrections.

Before going farther I will briefly describe the principal characteristics of the islands we are about to visit. The Hawaiian Islands are situated in the west Pacific Ocean. They lie between 18° 50′ and 22° 20′ north latitude, between 154° 53′ and 160° 15′ west longitude from Greenwich. The islands are eight in number: Hawaii, Maui, Oahu, Kanai, Malokai, Lanai, Niihau, and Kahoolawe. The three latter are comparatively unimportant. This group was named the Sandwich Islands on their discovery by Captain Cook, in honor of his patron, the Earl of Sandwich, then First Lord of the Admiralty.

The following table may be of interest, although I shall go but little into statistics, as the annual reports issued by the Hawaiian Government will furnish more details than this volume is intended to give.

Island.	Greatest Length Miles.	Greatest Breadth Miles.	Number of Square Miles.	Number Acres.	Population, Census of 1890.	Highest Elevation Feet.
Hawaii,	90	73	4,210	2,500,000	26,784	13,805
Maui,	48	30	760	400,000	17,357	10,032
Oahu,	46	25	600	360,000	31,194	4,060
Kanai,	22	25	590	350,000	11,859	4,800
Molokai,	40	7	270	200,000	2,632	3,500
Lanai,	17	9	150	100,000	174	3,000
Niihau,	20	7	97	70,000	. . .	800
Kahoolawe,	11	8	63	30,000		1,450

The highest peaks in the Island of Oahu:

	Feet.
Kaala,	4,030
Palikea, Waianae Mountains,	3,111
Konahuanui Peak, south of Pali,	3,106
Lanihuli Peak, north of Pali,	2,780
Diamond Head, Leahi,	762
Koko Head,	1,206

Island of Maui:

Haleakala,	10,032

Island of Hawaii:

Mauna Kea,	13,805
Mauna Loa,	13,675
Hualalai,	8,275

Population, 1890:

Natives,	34,436
Half castes,	6,186
Chinese,	15,301
Americans,	1,928
Hawaiian born, foreign parents,	7,495
Japanese,	12,360
Norwegians,	227
Britons,	1,344
Portuguese,	8,602
Germans,	1,034
French,	70
Other foreigners,	419
Polynesian,	588
Total,	89,990

In 1894 the schools numbered 176.

In 1895:

In Government schools, . . . 260 teachers,	9,264 pupils
In independent schools, . . . 175 "	3,375 "
Total, ... 435 "	12,639 "

Owing to the coral reefs there are no really good harbors except Honolulu and Pearl Harbor.

The islands are of volcanic structure. On the island of Hawaii is found the largest known active volcano, and several others of great size, partially or wholly quiescent.

There are many plains with soil composed of ashes and cinders. Extinct volcanoes of every age, size, and shape are common. One of these is a well-known promontory near Honolulu called Leahi, better known as Diamond Head, from an idea once current that precious stones were to be found there.

There are few minerals. The usual varieties of lava and pumice stone are found. No metals have been discovered. The soil of the islands is formed of decomposed volcanic rocks, sand, mud, and ashes; to be made fertile it requires constant irrigation.

The fruits are the banana, bread fruit, cocoanut, strawberry, raspberry, the ohia, a red, juicy mountain apple, melons, limes, oranges, guavas, pineapples, grapes, figs, peaches, citron; while rice, coffee, cotton, indigo, tobacco, and sugar-cane are successfully raised; also yams, sweet potatoes, and arrow root.

The forests are usually very dense, broken here and there by deep chasms, which appear to have been once active craters. The trees are overgrown with mosses and ferns, which render penetration almost impossible.

HAWAIIAN HOTEL, HONOLULU.

Wild geese, ducks, plover, hogs, dogs, steers, and wild horses abound in the islands.

The climate is salubrious, and the temperature even. During twelve years the greatest heat in the shade was ninety degrees, greatest cold fifty-four. The mean temperature is about seventy-five.

It is said that a stranger, asking a resident if the climate of the islands was favorable for lung troubles, was told that some three years ago a Chinaman settled in Honolulu with one lung, and recently returned to his native country with three lungs (his wife and two children).

The history of the people is too well known for me to enter into its details.

We are driven to the Hawaiian Hotel, a plain, unpretentious wooden structure, surrounded by a beautiful lawn, with palms, bananas, and other tropical trees and plants of magnificent foliage, rendering it a veritable paradise, with which we fall in love at first sight. Comfortable quarters are assigned us, and we are soon off to slumber and happy dreams amid the sweet odors that fill the air. Mosquitoes and other winged pests exist here to an alarming extent. All sleeping apartments are protected by netting, otherwise these energetic and persistent creatures would prove intolerable. Many hotels have what is called a " mosquito room ;" the sides are made of netting, which these insects cannot pass.

Mark Twain said that when on a visit to these islands, the only way to get the better of the " dear little humming birds," was to cut a hole in the netting, then get into bed; the mosquitoes would come through in droves; at the proper moment he would tie up the hole, get out of bed, and sleep unmolested on the floor.

Our first meal in this strange country is breakfast. The tables are filled with native fruits, such as alligator pears, bananas, pineapples, apples, and last, but not least, the universal dish called "poi."

TARO PATCH, HONOLULU.

I must speak more particularly of this article of food, which is so extensively used on the islands by residents as well as natives. Poi is made of the root of the taro plant, which, having been soaked and the skin removed, is dried and powdered; water is then poured on it, and it is set aside to ferment, or, in other words, until it becomes sour, at which time it assumes the consistency of paste. It is then ready to be eaten. At the hotels it is served like mush, and eaten with sugar and cream, or pressed hard and taken in a solid form, with butter and salt. It is a tasteless, unpalatable sort of food, but considered quite wholesome.

MAKING POI.

After breakfast we start out sightseeing. Walking to one of the principal streets, upon which there is a line of cars, we enter one. Such an odd, old-fashioned affair! The car has an oval top, and is as wide as a yacht. It is drawn by a pair of dilapidated old mules, apparently fed on air. Our destination is the noted Waikiki Beach, three miles distant.

We leave our unpleasantly rolling and rocking vehicle gladly, to wander along the beach. Here we find bath-houses, so, donning the suit usually worn by the men, a pair of swimming trunks, I plunge into the ocean, and enjoy the mild temperature and fine surf. The reef, about two miles seaward, protects this inland bay, where the swimmer may enjoy a frolic with old Neptune unmolested by the thousands of carnivorous sharks which inhabit these waters.

Many thrilling stories are told of the experiences of the natives with these dreaded fish. A Kanaka will often row his boat out beyond the reef, and, seeing a shark, will dive into the water and engage in battle with him; and it is always the Kanaka who kills his enemy.

Surf boating is one of the many pleasures afforded by the sea, to resident as well as native. Through the kindness of my good friend, Colonel McF——, I am invited to join in one of these novel sports. The canoes used are very long and narrow, being kept in place upon the water by two long outriders which support a heavy timber. Our party, consisting of my friend, three native Kanakas, and myself, dressed in bathing costume, and each provided with a paddle, row out to the reef, where the waves are high and powerful. Here we await one unusually large and strong. When such a one appears, and we hear it hissing in our ears, with its white crest close upon us, we begin to paddle all together towards the shore; as soon as the wave strikes the canoe we are carried with great speed upon its crest, at the rate of fully a mile a minute. We reach the beach alive and unharmed.

SURF BOATING, HONOLULU.

This is a very exciting and sometimes dangerous amusement, for, while the canoe cannot sink, it often capsizes, throwing its occupants into the water, where the force of the waves is so great as to render swimming a hazardous experiment. The sport is repeated many times until fatigue ends our enjoyment.

One day while sitting on the beach reveling in the beauty of picturesque Diamond Head, and the tropical plants and trees that fringe the shore, I observe a party, consisting of two young girls and a very old woman, each carrying a salt sack carelessly at her side, enter the water, and swim at least half a mile seaward. Then they dive, and remain a long time under water. I time some of these dives, and perceive that fully two minutes elapse before they return to the surface. They are gathering sea moss, and having filled their bags, swim ashore with the precious load. This moss is eaten by the Kanakas, and is quite palatable. The old woman is at least ninety years of age, and an athlete in strength.

The drive to Waikiki Beach is most charming. Along the entire way, on either side are picturesque and elegant mansions, set in lawns filled with tropical plants, royal palms, banana and cocoanut groves, and flowers in profusion. What a region of loveliness! The air is full of fragrance, the scenes are those of fairyland.

We have passed many large banana and cocoanut groves, and seen hundreds of cocoanuts and bunches of bananas awaiting the harvest.

It is very entertaining to take an open carriage and drive to the various stores. Passing through the principal streets, we enter a Japanese store, where I purchase a native island straw hat; also a large fancy sash, called a "puggery," which is to be draped artistically around the hat. Odd at first, but when one becomes familiar with it, quite the thing, and "swell" Honolulu style. With a white flannel or linen suit,

WAIKIKI BEACH, HONOLULU.

and white canvas shoes, one feels as if he has lived on these particular islands all his life.

We go from store to store, purchasing many articles, useful, convenient, and curious. Prices in general are the same as in the "States," but clothing of all kinds is much cheaper.

The tailors and dressmakers, nearly all Japanese or Chinese, are skilful workmen, and wonderfully quick in fulfilling orders. For instance, on Saturday at noon I telephone a Chinese tailor to bring samples of linen and flannel to our hotel, as we wish to order suits. He calls promptly with numerous styles of goods, at prices far below my calculations. They would be reasonable in our country at double the charge.

Choosing my materials, I order two suits, to be finished positively by Monday night. I do not really require them so soon, but do this as a joke and to put the tailor on his mettle. To my surprise, at supper time of the same day, his tailorship calls at the hotel, bearing upon his arm the two suits to be tried on, preparatory to finishing; and punctually on Monday evening I find awaiting me in my room the two suits of clothing and the smiling tailor, who asks politely if he is in good time.

It is worth while to take a stroll in the fish market, which is an open building, covering an acre and a half of ground; a lofty roof protects dealers and customers from the rays of the sun and the frequent showers for which Honolulu is noted.

The market is only ten minutes' walk from the hotel. I will never forget my first impressions of this curious scene. Sellers and buyers, of all nationalities—Kanakas, Chinese, Japanese, Portuguese,

English, and Americans—mingle together as one nation.

And such strange fish are on the table! One is of emerald green, one of purple, here a blue, there a black specimen.

Everywhere may be seen the voluptuous eyed Kanaka women, robed in their simple "Mother Hubbard" gowns, talking, laughing, merry-making, always bright and cheerful, and not only in the market, but at every turn of the street.

The dealers have an odd way of bundling up a fish and handing it to the purchaser without basket, string, or paper. They wrap two leaves, about eighteen inches long and five inches wide, dexterously around the fish, tie a knot, make an extra twist, and behold a basket with two handles, ingenious, primitive, and cheap.

To-day we visit the cricket grounds. The admission fee is twenty-five cents. Upon the grand stand are seated fully four hundred spectators and the celebrated Hawaiian Band of sixty pieces. Among the audience are many young half-breed Kanaka girls, of whose languishing eyes, handsome forms, and glowing health it is almost impossible to give an idea. The men, too, are perfect types of physical health and strength.

We spend an hour or two looking at a fairly good game of base-ball between the Kanaka club and a Cycle club, but find the music much more attractive than the play of amateurs.

In the evening, as I sit upon the porch listening to

"Hula" Dancers.

the music, and gazing out into the moonlit night and the tropical bloom surrounding the hotel, a party of gentlemen with whom I am acquainted approach and ask me if I will join them in witnessing a genuine "Hula" dance. I consent, and at eight o'clock we proceed, with a competent guide, to a neighboring cottage, where the dance is to be held. The dancing is odd and by no means beautiful.

These dances were instituted by the natives in their primitive life, as festivals to the Goddess Laka.

Returning to the hotel we are impressed by the gay and lovely picture of life it presents.

Parlor, reception and ballroom are beautiful and fragrant with flowers, and dozens of happy young people are gliding gracefully through the modern waltz, to the music of four Kanaka men, who sing and play at the same time. The instruments are a violin, banjo, and two guitars.

What a strange, sweet melody this native music has! So different from our own. As the dance goes on and on, and I sit on the porch smoking under the electric lights, with the dusky foliage around me, and the soft sweet melody ringing in my ears, I can almost believe that I have been transported from the everyday world to a true and living paradise.

PLANTATIONS AND MOUNTAINS.

Second-class cars—Native smokers—Rice plantation—Fields of sugar-cane—Crushing the cane—Planting cane—Lunch in a cocoanut grove—Pearl City and harbor—Pineapple farm—Chinese theatres—Strangers in Honolulu—Climate—Departure of the "Australia"—The Pali—On the summit—Ladies and the Pali—Punch Bowl—Photographing the natives—"Poi dog"—Crab fishing.

THIS fair morning I leave the city at nine o'clock with a party of gentlemen to visit the great sugar-cane plantations and pineapple farms at Pearl River and Waianae, the latter place nearly thirty-four miles from Honolulu.

In order to observe the natives we purchase second-class tickets at the railway station; the first-class cars are usually occupied by tourists and the better class of the inhabitants. We are well repaid for our choice. Opposite us is an old Kanaka woman and two young girls, all dressed in the loose "Mother Hubbard" garment.

After inspecting us closely, and seeming satisfied that we are harmless, the old woman reaches down into her deep pocket and draws forth an ancient pipe, rudely fashioned from a root; then a tobacco pouch. She fills the pipe, lights it and takes two or three puffs, then hands it to the young girl at her side, who also puffs several times, and passes the pipe to the other girl. With evident enjoyment it is thus smoked alternately until the tobacco is exhausted, when it is refilled and taken in turn as before.

There are numerous schools in Honolulu, and many of the Kanakas have been taught to speak the English language. We converse with some of these natives, who give us much information in regard to the country through which we are traveling. One of them, a handsome middle-aged Kanaka, educated at one of the Honolulu colleges, proves a very agreeable and interesting companion. He is a native of Waianae, and well acquainted with that portion of the island.

Our train consists of a first and a second-class car, and we travel at the rate of fifteen miles an hour on a fairly good track. As I look from my car window I see many uncommon and picturesque sights. On one side the mountains rise hundreds of feet, their summits ever enveloped in clouds; on the other the ocean waves dash ceaselessly upon a rugged coast.

The color effects on and around Oahu are the most beautiful I have ever beheld.

We stop now a few minutes at a station where a number of natives appear to receive letters and merchandise. These simple folk are interesting from the fact that they know and care almost nothing for the outside world.

Close by is a Japanese fish house; it is of two stories. Many of the men are loitering about between working hours. Their dress is odd and unbecoming.

We pass a rice plantation, on which many men are employed. Over in a distant corner I see a native buffalo harnessed to a plough. Buffaloes are commonly used throughout this district. The soil is a perfect mush, and the costume of the laborers is a loose blouse, minus trousers. The ground here is irrigated; the farms are owned by the railroad company and leased to the planters. I endeavor to learn the rate per acre, but without success. The rice is quite short, having been only recently planted. Here are also many fields of taro.

The railroad runs for miles along the base of the Waianae Mountains, which abound in wild pigs, dogs, and goats. By paying a small license fee one may have the privilege of hunting here to his heart's content. The mountains are of volcanic formation, composed chiefly of basalt.

We have reached Waianae, and in company with our new acquaintance, Mr. Haiakulani, and by his courtesy we are allowed to go through a large sugar mill. On our journey thither we passed miles upon miles of sugar-cane fields belonging to the company owning this mill. The cane is ripe, and a large force of men is employed in cutting it. After it is cut it is carried by small cars over a narrow track running from the field to the crushing-mill, and is here unloaded into hoppers, and the juice extracted by large powerful rollers. It passes through the rollers three times, the liquid being conveyed to a central point, and into a large trough

SUGAR-CANE FIELD.

with a copper sieve at the bottom, through which it is strained. It is then carried to large tubs at the top of the mill, where the molasses and sugar are made. Huge piles of crude brown sugar run through spouts upon the floor beneath, and are bagged for shipment by the natives. The molasses is shipped in hogsheads.

The refuse cane is dried and used for fuel, thus serving a threefold purpose.

Cane is planted by cutting a canestalk, sixteen or eighteen inches long, and planting it a few inches below the surface of the earth; a young stalk sprouts from each joint or eye. Its luxuriant growth can easily be imagined. In fourteen months from planting it reaches maturity, sometimes attaining a height of twenty feet.

Leaving the sugar mill, we stroll over to one of the many cocoanut groves in the neighborhood to lunch and rest under the shady trees and enjoy the view. The proprietor of the grove invites us to help ourselves to as many green cocoanuts as we wish, to eat with our lunch. We take this as a joke, as the trees are tall and the fruit very high; but in a few moments a small Kanaka lad, not over ten years of age, comes running toward us, sent by the owner to climb one of the trees and knock down cocoanuts for us!

How nimble these Kanaka boys are! With perfect ease he runs up a tree fifty or sixty feet high, and with his feet knocks down as many cocoanuts as we desire.

The fruit being green, one can easily cut off the top and drink the milk. It is delicious. I think each cocoanut contains about three pints of milk.

Returning to Waianae Station, we say farewell to our kind friend and guide, and take the train for Pearl City.

Here we ascend a high hill, not far from the station, to obtain a bird's-eye view of the famous Pearl Harbor. How restful to eyes and soul is this beautiful body of water!

During our walk we meet a native, who, upon inquiry, tells us that only a mile or two distant is one of the largest pineapple farms in the neighborhood. Taking him as our guide, we start for the plantation.

Arriving shortly, we are fortunate enough to find the wife of the proprietor at home. She welcomes us hospitably, and leads us to the large tract of ground entirely devoted to the cultivation of this fruit. It is an interesting sight. Here are thousands of pineapples nearly ready for the market. This farm will produce one hundred and fifty thousand pineapples in one crop, averaging ten thousand to the acre. Artesian wells are made and the soil is irrigated. The price of pineapples from first hands is about ten cents apiece, regardless of size; their weight is from seven to twelve pounds, although I have seen much fruit weighing fully fifteen to eighteen pounds. The fruit appears twelve months after the bud is planted and matures two months later. What a feast we had before leaving the plantation! We return to Honolulu, feeling well repaid for our trip.

In the evening we attend a Chinese theatre—in fact, two theatres. The city maintains two theatres, both under the management of the Chinese. One is called the "Old" the other the "New" theatre. There is little or no difference between them, either inside or out. The audience, which is composed of Japanese and Chinese, seems to be most interested in that part of the performance which makes the greatest noise; the continuous beating of large gongs and brass cymbals, which is something dreadful!

The stranger visiting Honolulu, if he is well recommended by letters of introduction, is cordially received in the best circles.

The people are hospitable and attentive in their entertainment of a visitor. The service at the hotel is also all that could be desired. The labor is performed entirely by Chinamen. Our chamber boy, "Ah Cue," seems happy only when fulfilling our orders, nothing that we ask being too much trouble.

While the climate is tropical the temperature is not high; yet the atmosphere has a relaxing effect, and one soon loses his "American vim" and energy, becoming, like natives and residents, quite willing to take things "easy."

The "Australia" is the favorite steamer of the people of Honolulu, and it is entertaining to go down to the harbor and witness her departure on one of her voyages.

The Hawaiian Band assembles on the end of the pier, playing popular and patriotic airs, while friends and relatives bid each other farewell on the steamer and the shore. Upon these occasions the natives bring long garlands of flowers, called "leis," four or five feet in length, which they place in lavish profusion about the necks and shoulders of the departing travelers. Just before the steamer casts off her moorings wreaths and

THE PALI ROAD.

flowers are flung over her in perfect abandon, shouts of "bon voyage!" mingle with cheers, music, and singing, and the excitement is intense.

We choose a clear, bright afternoon for our drive to the celebrated Pali, six miles and a half from Honolulu. The road is a gradual ascent to a height of over twelve hundred feet above the level of the sea, with mountains towering on either side from three thousand to four thousand feet high. As we ascend the scenery continually increases in grandeur, the foliage grows more dense, and the air perceptibly cooler. The gently-sloping sides of the valley have changed to lofty precipices. We mount higher and higher, over a good road, passing at intervals other travelers.

Before us is a group of Kanakas, men and women, riding their horses bareback and in one fashion. Here are some Japanese and Chinamen, also en route for the Pali.

At a picturesque turn in the path we perceive an artist at work upon his canvss. The scene grows more and more beautiful as we still move upward, almost on the edge of a steep precipice. Now we tie the horses and leave the carriage at a spot protected by the mountain from the strong wind which never ceases in this region. Walking several hundred feet, at a sudden turn we come to the very edge of the precipice. The strong iron railing is a necessary protection here, for the wind is furious, threatening to sweep everything before it.

The natives frequently ride over this bridle path and down the steep mountain side to the plain below.

The view from this point is magnificent. Lofty mountains tower far, far above us on all sides, their

80   VACATION DAYS IN HAWAII AND JAPAN.

peaks, covered with verdure, lending an indescriable majesty to the scene.

Away off on the right can be seen the Pacific Ocean spreading its calm surface mile upon mile, its emerald coat glistened brightly in the sun. Along the coast

Now we Tie the Horses.

white foam above the coral reefs indicates shallow water.

The plains, with their varied hues of green and brown, in light and shadow, show now brilliant, now softened effects of richest coloring.

Here, where we stand, a great battle was fought a

hundred years ago, and Kamehameha, the conqueror, drove his enemies over the edge of this frightful precipice to their death.

Far off, yet almost directly opposite, is the little rocky island of Molokai, with steep rugged sides.

We gaze around us, breathless with wonder, and too deeply impressed for words. The wind, roaring through the pass, adds to the feeling of awe with which we are inspired. It is sometimes even more violent, and we are told that frequently large stones from the valley are lifted by it with such force that they are carried to the top of this pass.

The ledge upon which we are standing is from fifteen to eighteen hundred feet above the plain.

The great Pali stands majestic and defiant, fearing neither the stormy winds nor the rushing waters. With royal grace it rears its beauteous head. Yet not always has it presented to the world so calm a front. Evidences of volcanic explosions are in the rocky mountain side, and, while one half stands in semicircular form the other half has sunk out of view, appearing as if cut away with mathematical precision.

We linger long among these most wonderful of the Creator's works. At length we return to the carriage, and are soon descending the picturesque valley of Nuuanu.

I take many photographs of the mountains and the

prospects along this drive; but what can art do, but give one a faint idea of the grandeur and sublimity of nature in her loftiest moods.

A story is told here of two ladies and the Pali. While staying at the hotel in Honolulu they received an invitation to the Queen's reception at the palace.

THE GREAT PALI STANDS MAJESTIC AND DEFIANT.

As evening approached they ordered a carriage, and wishing to air their French they directed the driver to take them to the "palais." The man, astonished at receiving such an order at that hour, asked if he understood aright, and the command was repeated: "To the palais."

They set out, and after riding a long time the ladies began to think the driver had either misunderstood them or lost his way. Signs of civilization were rapidly disappearing. As they entered the mountain pass they asked him if he knew the road. He replied, by asking in his turn, if they wished to go to the Pali. They said they did. So on they went, until at last the Pali was reached—a bleak wilderness at that hour. When informed that they had arrived at the Pali, they were amazed and alarmed, and asked the driver where was the palace of the queen? To which he answered, "Not here; this is the Pali." Angry and mortified, they were driven back to the hotel, having missed the reception at the palace.

A delightful drive is to the Punch Bowl, and along the coast. Ordering a carriage, we direct the driver to take us to the summit of this extinct crater, which rises five hundred feet above the valley. Upon reaching this elevation, we have a fine view of Diamond Head, also an extinct crater, and in the distance of the lofty Waianae Mountains, with a pure blue sky for a background. From another point we can see Pearl Harbor.

At our feet is the harbor of Honolulu, with steamers lying at anchor, and merchandise of all kinds awaiting shipment to foreign lands, piled upon the piers, which extend far into the sea. We have also a beautiful view of the city of Honolulu. Descending, we drive through the bed of the crater, which is covered with a dense growth of lowly verdure.

Many native houses and grass huts are built upon the mountain side. Wishing to see some of the people in their homes, we direct the driver, who speaks the Kanaka language, to stop before some of these dwell-

A DELIGHTFUL DRIVE IS TO THE PUNCH BOWL.

ings. The first is a small grass hut, whose inhabitants I ask to come out that I may photograph them. They are very shy at first, but finally an old man and a boy pose for me while engaged in eating poi. In extending a coin to the man to repay him for the favor, I discover that he is a leper; his face, hands, and the ex-

PLANTATIONS AND MOUNTAINS. 85

Many Native Houses and Grass Huts are Built upon the Mountain Side.

posed portions of his body are covered with evidences of this loathsome disease. I drop the money into his swollen palm and turn away.

At another hut the family is preparing for a feast, called " Poi Dog." The Kanakas frequently have these entertainments. A dog is penned up and fattened upon poi, then killed, cooked, and served much as we serve a young pig in our country.

We now drive along the beach, passing Diamond Head and Koko Point. Halting at a retired and shady spot, we spread leaves upon the ground, and eat our luncheon sitting upon the rocks.

Then, still along the shore, homeward. By this time the tide is coming rapidly in, and the huge boulders on our right and the water on our left are so close together that at times the horses are compelled to wade breast high through the surf. We have a very exciting ride for about two miles. Now and then a wave breaks so close to us that we are drenched with spray.

During our drive we pass the residences of many prominent people, among them the cottages of President Dole and the ex-Queen Liliuokalani. Arriving home, we find that we have been out six hours.

Our kind friend, Colonel McF——, invites us, with others, to a crab-fishing picnic. Many island celebrities are to be there, and we anticipate much fun.

Carriages await us at the hotel at eleven in the morning.

Driving to Kalihi, a distance of four miles, we are hospitably received by our host at his summer residence.

Provided with fishing tackle and raw beef for bait we all repair to the beach, where we have much sport and catch some fine large crabs. We then return to the farm, where we enjoy an *al fresco* dinner.

The rustic table under the trees is bountifully laden with choice dishes, such as roast duck, beefsteak, bread fruit, alligator pears, cakes, and beer. To crown all, the Chinese cook appears, bearing a huge dish of the crabs we have caught, prepared for dinner.

The cool breeze from the ocean and the delightful, balmy atmosphere, with just enough sun, make the meal a charming success. The aspect is enchanting. On our right rises Mount Tantalus, two thousand feet above us, and covered with verdure to its highest point.

Choice cigars finish the repast, and many a good story is told as we recline luxuriously in easy chairs and hammocks.

The sociability of the residents adds greatly to the pleasure of the tourist. Long will I remember the crab fishing picnic at Kalihi.

To-day is devoted to preparation for our journey to

Hilo and the crater of Kilauea on the island of Hawaii. The distance by sea is about two hundred miles. We leave to-morrow on the steamer "Kinau."

We have a pleasant habit of spending an hour after breakfast on the porch in front of the hotel, where are exposed for sale various specimens of the handicraft of the natives and others.

Bead-work, baskets, bags, and belts made of the seeds of fruits; also lace mats are offered by the Portuguese. Fans made of dried grasses, wooden figures carved in primitive style with a jack-knife, and many other curious articles may be bought at a moderate price.

THE HOUSE OF EVERLASTING FIRE.

Off for Hilo—Old Neptune's frolics—Views en voyage—Lanai—Landing cargo—Temple of Haen—Niulii—Mountain waterfalls—Loupahoehoe—Hilo—Unpleasant bedfellows—Drive to the crater—Flume bridges—Native jungles—Japanese moving—Halfway House—Volcano Hotel—The crater of Halemaumau—Kilauea—Mauna Kea—Walk to the crater—Lava formations—The House of Everlasting Fire—Candle tree—Bird's nest fern—Return to Hilo—American circus—Cocoanut Island—Kanaka church—Native bathers—Back to Honolulu.

Mr. W——, president of the Wilder Line of steamships, has most kindly given up his stateroom to us during the voyage. This is only one of many favors extended to us by the officers of this company, for which we will ever be grateful.

We leave the Wilder pier at 10.30 on a bright sunny morning.

Many friends are gathered on the shore to see us off and wish us a safe journey.

We pass Diamond Head shortly after leaving the harbor, having a fine view of the picturesque coast, with its luxuriant foliage, from the deck of the steamer.

The Pacific, while placid in name, is capable at times of showing a rough and unpleasant disposition, and this proves to be our experience in the early part of the voyage. We begin to roll considerably as we pass through the Kaiwi channel, and with the exception of two gentlemen all the passengers are seasick. In all my experience at sea I have never seen the ocean as rough as in this channel.

Even the president of the line declares that he has never passed through anything equal to this.

The islands of Molokai and Maui loom up majestically before us, and I forget my sufferings for a moment in admiration of the charming picture. The setting sun shows a golden light in a deep purple background, and the waves glisten with orange and violet reflections; now a rich crimson glow spreads over all, which gradually fading, leaves our memory sole possessors of a scene of beauty indelibly impressed upon its tablets.

We cast anchor and bob up and down in midstream. We can see the old town of Lahaina upon the island of Maui, fully a mile away. Small boats are let down from the steamer's side to convey passengers and freight ashore. While this is being accomplished I lean over the side of the vessel, at the suggestion of Mr. W——, to observe the clearness of the water, and at a depth of sixty feet can distinguish shells as well as fish. I cast a silver coin into the waves and watch it zigzag its way down to the bottom of the sea.

The row boats, having landed passengers and stores, are hoisted into place, and again we are moving onward.

What a gale! The sea is uncomfortably restless, and our little steamer seems anxious to perform the undesirable feat of standing on her head.

The scenery along the route is sublime. Mr. W—— invites us to the bridge to view the great mountains of Maui. The giant Haleakala, in all the dignity of its ten thousand and thirty-two feet, looks wild and barren. Little or no vegetation clothes its topmost peaks; but at its base there is a luxuriant growth of tropical foliage. Through the twilight we can perceive fields of sugar-cane and little white cottages dotted here and there, with the tall mountains for a background. The enchanting scenes that pass in rapid panorama almost banish the headache and nausea.

Here is "Olowalu," pleasant valley, well deserving its name. The green fields of cane, the gently rolling country in its emerald robe would be a veritable Arcadia, were it not for the occasional appearance of a sugar mill, with which the speculative spirit of man has seen fit to mar the harmony of this lovely spot.

We are informed that the island of Lanai, lying before us, is for sale, being in a state of bankruptcy It may be purchased for ninety thousand dollars; it has good pasture land for sheep and cattle.

It is long after midnight before I retire to my stateroom, leaving reluctantly these lovely pictures of sea and mountain. But what a place do I enter! This is more like the dwelling of a cyclone than the berth of a steamer. Nearly everything in the room—books, grips, tumblers, what not?—has found a resting place on the floor. The utmost confusion prevails.

I tie myself in bed and yield myself up to the possibilities of slumber. I have just fallen asleep, when I am aroused by the persistent squealing of pigs. Not understanding the necessity for such sounds at this unseemly hour, I rise and make my way to the deck, where I perceive that we have anchored opposite Makena, and are transferring passengers and freight, pigs, ashore.

It is a glorious night! The moon shining on the water calls forth myriads of sparkling diamonds. Wind and waves have subsided considerably, and, although we are still tossing about, it is not impossible to sleep. The steward informs me, however, that we may expect another "shake up" when we pass through the Alenuihaha channel. Merciful heavens! I retire to bed with dismal visions of another bone-rattling!

Bang! Bang! Bang? Now a dish; now a glass crashing on the floor awakens me. And such tossing and pitching can be compared only to a cowboy upon a bucking broncho, and a spirited one at that. I fall twice from my berth, and only by strapping myself in can I save myself from being again deposited upon the floor. At seven o'clock in the morning we arrive at

Mahukona, the first landing on the island of Hawaii, where we will remain three hours, while freight is being conveyed ashore.

Mr. W—— invites us to land and breakfast with himself and family at his country residence close by. The boat is lowered and passengers are rowed ashore by natives.

Upon an eminence at our right a pretty cottage is perched, surrounded by plenty of shade trees. Here we receive a warm welcome and a good breakfast.

After breakfast I walk to the wharf to see the unloading of the cargo. As before, the steamer lies a mile from shore, and the fright is placed in boats and rowed to its destination, large timbers being thrown overboard and towed to the land. Live cattle, such as steers and horses, are lowered into the water and swim ashore.

Mahukona is a barren-looking place, although in certain sections there are large sugar plantations. It is about one hundred and twenty miles from Honolulu and eighty from Hilo, our destination.

With the good wishes of our hosts we say farewell, and our steamer goes on her way.

Shortly after leaving Mahukona we see upon a bank a large pile of stones, and we are told that it is the ruins of the once famous temple of Haen, built by the Goddess Genii. Many human sacrifices were made

within its walls by the ancient kings, and there are
numerous traditions relating to it. One is that the
sacred shrine was raised by the goddess in a single
night.

The island of Hawaii is not so mountainous as Maui.
There is much excellent pasture here and cattle ranches

These Flumes are Carried Over Deep Valleys.

abound. Numerous herds may be seen grazing, some
of them numbering hundreds of heads.

This is also a sugar-cane district, and here are large
plantations and many mills. The cane, when cut, is
conveyed to the mills by means of troughs or flumes,
into which water is forced. These flumes are carried

over deep valleys, from three hundred to four hundred feet below, before reaching the mills.

We see a number of square inclosures, of small size, surrounded by stone walls, long since in ruins, and are informed that at one time the natives lived there; but so many of them died that the remainder deserted their homes, proving that the first attempts at civilization were not successful among the aborigines. The exquisite scenery, as we approach the Niulii district, is beyond a hasty description. I have taken several photographs of the beautiful lofty mountains that cast their shadows over the water, and, had we sailed more smoothly, would attempt some sketches, but it is impossible under existing conditions.

As we advance the scenes are grander, more inspiring. The mountains tower two thousand feet from the very edge of the sea, while in the background rise the peaks, Kohala, five thousand five hundred feet, and Mauna Kea, thirteen thousand eight hundred feet. The loftier mountains seem to be guarding their lesser neighbors in the foreground.

I have no words adequate to these wonderful heights and depths and lights and shadows and rich and softened hues of tropical wealth and bloom. These summits, it is said, have never been trodden by foot of man. I can well believe this statement, as they are extremely precipitous.

Although covered by trees and other vegetation there are no wild animals upon them. The gigantic masses are broken here and there by deep, mysterious looking ravines that fill one with awe. Cascades shoot forth from inner heights at an elevation of from a thousand to fifteen and even eighteen hundred feet, dashing over the precipices into the sea, and forming innumerable rainbows in the glistening sunlight.

A few grass huts are scattered at the base of the mountains, the abodes of fishermen, whose little boats are their only means of communication with the outside world. There is no road except at the foot of the mountains, and when the weather is bad and the sea rough they are frequently unable to leave their homes for many weeks.

Hawaii is quite fertile in this district, as we see many sugar plantations which extend from the shore to the woodlands.

As we approach Laupahoehoe the mountains are smaller. Here we land some passengers.

We are now only twenty-one miles from Hilo, at which place we hope to arrive at 5.30 this afternoon. The country here is wild and picturesque, great waves dashing high upon a rocky beach.

We can see Hilo in the distance, a small insignificant looking place, of tropical appearance.

At last we make our final halt, the boats are lowered

for the last time, and we are all borne safely to a primitive wharf, where we are met by natives and driven to the Volcano Hotel.

We are well received by "mine host," who offers us the best in his house, which is as poor as he is generous.

We take the parlor, in which a bed is placed, and with a small pitcher of water manage a tolerably fair appearance at our first meal on shore, which is supper.

As I finish the day's journal, and just before retiring for the night, the porch is surrounded by Kanakas, who favor us with native songs, accompanied by musical instruments. Their voices sound as though some " Brown's Troches " would not be injurious.

I retire to rest, anticipating a good sleep. My first impression is that a blanket has been thrown over the backs of two or three camels, and that I am lying on it. Anything more uneven than these springs it is impossible to imagine.

We have also many unpleasant bed-fellows, such as fleas innumerable, myriads of mosquitoes, enormous spiders, sociable centipedes. In time one becomes accustomed to these creatures, which are quite common to the sleeping-rooms of this part of the country. The spiders are really remarkable; when standing, their legs are from four to six inches long. They are, however, harmless, and are never killed by the natives, as they are great destroyers of fleas and other annoying insects. Two of these great fellows remain quietly in our canopy through the night, doubtless to protect us from evils, of whose existence we are not aware. Thank heaven, the night is past! But it has left many souvenirs upon our bodies.

After breakfast we start on our thirty-mile drive to the crater of Kilauea, engaging a private carriage in preference to the stage which runs between these points. The road, composed of lava, was constructed by the Hawaiian government in 1894 at a cost of one hundred thousand dollars.

Fields of sugar-cane extend for miles along the way on either side. It is estimated that in the district of Hilo fifty thousand acres are devoted to this product, half of it being cropped each year. Formerly the cane was hauled to the mills in carts, requiring the service of thousands of mules and oxen. Now all this work is accomplished by the flumes, many of which are from five to eight miles long, frequently crossing, as I have already said, deep and wide ravines. One of the longest and highest of these is more than fifteen hundred feet long and from two hundred to two hundred and fifty feet high. Rain is so abundant in Hilo that the planters use it for transporting the cane through the flumes, thus saving the cost of artesian wells.

It is said that in Hawaii one must be prepared for a

shower at any moment. We find this to be true. The natives declare that it rains eight days in every week.

We are now in a dense forest, where the trees meet overhead, and tropical plants of every description abound. Graceful ferns spring up on all sides, and vines, bearing brilliant-hued flowers, climb the trees and festoon the branches with gay wreaths. Wild oranges, bananas, and other southern fruits gleam through the leaves, and strange vegetation thrusts toward us grotesque shapes and peculiar foliage. Only one thing is lacking in this region of lavish and wondrous growth. Scarcely a note proclaims the presence of the sweet musician of the wood, here, where one would expect to find the feathered songster in his most gorgeous plumage. The birds seem to be supplanted by the enormous spiders which abound everywhere.

The traveler in the States cannot fail to notice the dozens of birds always perched upon the telegraph wires. Here hundreds of spiders, of every size, may be seen hanging to the wires anxiously watching for their prey.

Several coffee plantations appear on the way. The trees producing this berry are small and pretty. Now follows a stretch of uncultivated land, covered with ferns and underbrush. Here and there an enterprising settler has cleared away a few acres and built himself a cozy little cottage.

We meet many Japanese men and women on the road, the men carrying all their household goods upon their backs. A long pole is balanced upon the shoulders, and the goods suspended from the ends. One passes us, bearing thus his cooking utensils, bed and bedding, and provisions. With this load he has one free hand, devoted to no better purpose than holding a cigar, which seems to afford him much pleasure.

We are not far enough from civilization to be out of reach of the bicycle, for a tandem has just passed us, with two riders, on their way to the crater Kilauea. Four times we meet them, and each time they call out to us that they have " punctured their tires."

Another tropical jungle, miles in extent, from which we emerge into a picturesque region, with the great giants Mauna Kea and Mauna Loa looking down upon us. We pass few residences.

It is now ten o'clock in the morning, and we have just reached the Halfway House at Olaa, where we change horses and lunch, stopping a half-hour. We have traveled sixteen miles since leaving Hilo.

On the road again, passing innumerable fern hedges enclosing the small lawns of diminutive cottages. Another forest, so dense that it seems almost impossible to penetrate it. Wild ferns abound in an endless variety; also the wild orange, banana, and guava.

As the soil here is composed of lava, there is but

little vegetation, and the remainder of the drive is without much interest. At 2.30 P. M. we arrive at the Volcano Hotel, which is situated on an elevation of four thousand feet and forty feet above sea-level, and three miles and a half from the crater of Halemaumau.

It is morning, and I sit upon the porch of the hotel

ANOTHER FOREST, SO DENSE THAT IT SEEMS IMPOSSIBLE TO PENETRATE IT.

gazing at the scene before me. On the west is the lofty Mauna Loa, with its highest point extending far above the clouds that circle about its head. This mountain is thirteen thousand six hundred and seventy-five feet high, and is the second in height upon the islands. It can be ascended on foot, but this is rarely attempted.

THE HOUSE OF EVERLASTING FIRE. 103

Upon its summit is the inactive crater Mokuaweoweo, which was last in operation April 24th, 1896. On the side of the mountain, four thousand feet above sea level, are the craters Kilauea and Halemaumau, the former inactive, the latter in operation.

From the rear of the hotel can be seen Mauna Kea,

OFF IN THE DISTANCE CAN BE SEEN SMOKE ARISING FROM THE CRATER HALEMAUMAU.

the highest mountain upon the Hawaiian group. It rises heavenward thirteen thousand eight hundred and five feet.

Off in the distance, some three miles, looking over the great lava beds of the crater Kilauea, can be seen smoke rising from the crater Halemaumau. On first appearance, and in looking at it from the porch of the hotel, one is apt to form a very poor estimate of the grandeur of this crater, and like many of nature's wonders, the tourist feels disappointed, after the long and fatiguing journey from Honolulu to Hilo, to witness the greatest of all active craters.

It is well to make a brief detail of this crater, Halemaumau. On December 7th, 1894, there were three lakes in action in this crater, and upon the above night these three lakes united, and fell to a depth of six hundred feet. The crater then became inactive until July 8th, 1896, at which time a roaring was heard, and the first notice of the crater being again active was July 11th, 1896. The crater is, say, five hundred feet deep and covers an area of three hundred feet in diameter, and is located in the great lava beds of the crater Kilauea; this latter crater covers an estimated area of nine miles in circumference.

At five o'clock in the afternoon, provided with stout walking-sticks, heavy shoes to protect our feet from the sharp points of lava, and waterproofs for the beating rain, we start for the crater. Some of the ladies use the small bony native horses for this trip. They are obliged to ride on men's saddles, as no others are to be had in this out-of-the-way place.

With guides at the front and rear of our party, we follow a narrow serpentine path, in Indian file, to the foot of the mountain, when we are within a few steps of the great lava bed of the crater Kilauea.

We tread cautiously upon this cold, black lava. What a sea of it stretches out before us! The path is

ONE OF THESE BUBBLES, BREAKING UNDER MY FEET, GIVES ME A TERRIBLE FRIGHT.

marked by piles of stones, two or three high, for there are many dangerous places into which we might stray. On either side of us are deep seams, varying from ten to twenty feet in depth. Even with the greatest care, one now and then treads upon a great bubble, whose thin crust breaks, and a fall of two or three feet is the consequence.

One of these bubbles, breaking under my feet, gives me a terrible fright. For a second my heart is in my mouth and my hair on end, for I know not where the fall will leave me.

Our walk over this plain is weird and silent, a hollow echo now and then warning us to tread more lightly or step aside upon a less aerial formation.

Many and wonderful are the shapes into which the lava has been forced. Here are great waves, with curling tops, apparently ready to break and crash against each other; here huge masses of rope lava, woven with more than human skill, and perfect to a fibre. No life is visible upon this dreary sea, save here and there an isolated fern, peeping out from a cold, black crevice, nods to us, as if gladly welcoming human visitors.

We push on and on with unfaltering steps, fearing even to pause, lest a crash ensue, and we be cast into eternity.

There is a long, deep fissure on our right, only a few steps from us. It is so wide and deep that a strong bridge has been placed over it. Steam puffs out of the numerous apertures, with a noise like that of an escape valve, filling the air with sulphurous odor. The heat is also perceptible through these openings. Night has fallen, and now the guides stop our party and provide each person with a lamp. We halt again at a corral made of lava stone, where the ladies dismount, and the horses are led within and tied. From this point, a distance of about half a mile, all must go afoot.

The heat from the crater is now oppressive, and we are compelled to remove our waterproofs. At last the

HUGE MASSES OF ROPE LAVA, WOVEN WITH MORE THAN HUMAN SKILL.

guides tell us that we are near the crater. Great columns of smoke are seen ascending hundreds of feet, a red glare flames up against the dark blue of the sky, and a low, deep rumbling falls upon our ears.

One is reminded of a scene in the "Inferno."

Louder and louder grows the rumbling noise, till the lava fairly roars in its fiery churn below. It is an awful scene! Darkness is everywhere, save where the "House of Everlasting Fire" sends forth its vivid illuminations.

As we draw nearer to the edge of the crater, our hearts beat more and more quickly. Now we are so close that great care is necessary to avoid slipping, or, by a careless movement, breaking the ledge on which we stand, and thus being all precipitated together into the fiery abyss. We seem like pilgrims at a shrine, as together we take our first look into the crater.

Is it possible to do justice to the grand spectacle?

With a temperature, estimated at 2,000 degrees, the molten lava hisses and tosses to and fro, sometimes assuming the form of huge billows whirling and dashing against each other in their mad rush back to the centre, at others pyramids and fiery fountains dart upward thirty or forty feet. There are intervals when the tumult ceases, and silence and darkness reign supreme. Then, as if by magic, the hot lava suddenly belches forth, waves roll upward, trying to outdo each other, fountains fling their fiery spray high in the air, clouds of smoke arise from the pit, and all is again aglow with crimson flame, while the roar grows more terrible every minute.

We gaze upon the scene in awed silence, almost

expecting an irresistible invitation from his sardonic majesty to take part in this royal festival.

When we return to the hotel, some three hours later, and our excited brains are beginning to cool, we all agree that we have seen one of the wonders of the world, and that the reality has far exceeded the anticipation in our visit to Halemaumau, "The House of Everlasting Fire."

We spend a few days visiting places of interest around the hotel, then return to Hilo.

I cannot dwell too often upon the delights of these forests. Here we see the Kukui, or Candle tree. The kernel from the nut of this tree is burned to give light. The natives also polish the nuts, and string them as beads. The ferns here grow to a height of twenty and thirty feet. The jungle is filled with a species of fern called Bird's Nest, which takes its name from the fact that it grows from the juncture of the bough with the tree, and resembles a bird's nest or a pot of ferns. The bark of the fern is six to eight inches thick, and is frequently cut into long strips, and used for making steps, and paving the private paths of the residents. The porous nature of the wood causes it to absorb water, and renders it soft and spongy under the feet. The atmosphere of the forest is like that of a hothouse: there is much moisture and the air is filled with aromatic odors.

We arrive at Hilo without event.

This evening, hearing that an "American Circus Company" is to give a performance in the town, I take advantage of the opportunity to observe the native element that will surely gather there. I enter the canvas tent at 8 o'clock, and receive a cordial greeting from the proprietor, who is one of my countrymen, and who is at the door collecting the tickets. He bids me pass on, free of charge, so I climb to the top row of seats, and wait till "the band begins to play."

Here is the usual queer, but happy mixture of the nationalities usually found in the islands: Japanese, Portuguese, Chinese, residents and natives.

Among the Kanakas are many women, young and old, smoking their pipes. The élite of the assembly are seated upon about thirty chairs, for which they have the privilege of paying a higher price than the others. An hour of the entertainment is as much as I can stand, and I surprise my friends on the porch of the hotel by my premature appearance among them.

After a restless night I find that Sunday is to be spent driving in a comfortable carriage to places of interest in the neighborhood.

Going in the direction of Cocoanut Island we have a fine view of the town of Hilo, which is snugly situated between her giant sentinels, Mauna Loa and Mauna Kea. On the first of these I can see plainly a barren, black streak running from the summit to within a mile of the city. This was caused by the flow of burning lava, thrown from the crater of the mountain in 1881, which nearly destroyed Hilo. After an hour's drive we stop and attend a native church service. The minister, a half-caste, speaks earnestly and fluently,

THE LOVELY AND PICTURESQUE COCOANUT ISLAND.

of course in the Kanaka tongue. After lunch we visit the lovely and picturesque Cocoanut Island, where we are surprised to see native women bathing in the harbor, utterly devoid of clothing. It is, however, a common thing for both men and women in this country to bathe thus.

The following morning we leave Hilo, amid cheers and farewells from friends and acquaintances assembled on the shore to see the steamer " Kinau " depart.

In consequence of a comparatively smooth sea and a heavy cargo, our return voyage is a delightful one. The weather is, with few exceptions, charming. We pass the lofty cliffs of Hamakua, with their numerous water-falls, and the charming valleys of Waimanu and Waipio, and after stopping at Mahukona, to land and receive freight, we bid a long farewell to the beautiful and romantic island of Hawaii.

We have a rough sea, crossing the channel. As we approach Lahaino, on the Island of Maui, the setting sun casts a glow of wonderful beauty over the scene. At this station a native brings some green cocoanuts on board the steamer; I partake of them, and find them quite palatable.

After an uneventful passage, we anchor at Honolulu on schedule time, having been away on our trip just a week.

FIRST IMPRESSION OF JAPAN.

Departure from Honolulu—The steamship "China"—Steerage passengers—Punkahas—Morning swim—Birds' Island—Collecting fares—Chinese gamblers—Letters of introduction—Chopsticks—Yokohama harbor—Chinese merchants—Japanese guide—Streets of Yokohama—Japanese theatre—The shampooer—A Jinrikisha ride—Japanese funeral—Mississippi Bay—Negishi—Tea house of Tsukimikan.

As we expect to sail for Yokohama, Japan, on the sixth of August, on the steamship "China," we spend the fifth in packing and making such purchases as may add to our comfort during the voyage of twelve days before us.

We rise bright and early on the day of sailing, and see upon the blackboard of the hotel that our steamer has arrived from San Francisco, and will leave for Yokohama at four o'clock this afternoon.

We are delighted with the appearance of the vessel. The Captain is a fine gentleman of magnificent physique, genial and kind, and master of his craft. The smiling faces of the first officer and purser make us feel at home, and with good friends.

And now we must say farewell to dear Honolulu and the kind friends who have done so much to make our stay here pleasant. They load us with sweet-scented "leis," which are placed around our heads and upon our necks and shoulders. It is a lovely send-off! We are sorry to part with them, and feel that although we have been only three weeks on the islands, we have made true and lasting friends.

At four o'clock the great propeller begins to agitate the water, and slowly and silently we leave behind us the ever beautiful land, so often and justly entitled "the Paradise of the Pacific."

Our steamer is a fine one in every respect, elegantly modeled, graceful and powerful. Her length is four hundred and sixty-five feet; drawing, when laden, twenty-six and one-half feet of water. Her beam amidship measures forty-nine feet nine inches, her tonnage is five thousand two hundred and fifty and her estimated cost one million dollars.

Order and cleanliness are everywhere manifest. The crew numbers one hundred and sixty-three, and is composed of thirty-four whites and one hundred and twenty-nine Chinamen.

One can form an idea of her size, when I state that sixteen times around her deck are equal to a mile. With the large white awnings to protect us from the heat of the sun and the cinders and smoke from the stack, we may in perfect comfort enjoy the delightful sea air and ocean view.

Glancing from our upper deck to the one below, we

FIRST IMPRESSION OF JAPAN. 115

perceive many of the steerage passengers eating their supper of rice, meat, and pickles. What adepts they are with their chopsticks! There are a few Chinese women and children among them. The children are cunning little tots, like the Chinese dolls we see in America. While we are observing these interesting people, the Captain joins us, and tells me that if I wish to take a swim in a tank sixteen feet long, by ten wide, and about six feet deep, I can do so in water drawn from the ocean. At first I think he is joking, but he shows me a huge canvas on the lower deck suspended from the rigging. "This," he says, "is filled every morning at five o'clock. A constant stream of water is pumped into the tank, and those of the cabin passengers who wish may take a swim." I tell him that I will gladly avail myself of this privilege.

There are many prominent persons on board, and as we sit at the Captain's table, we have an opportunity to make their acquaintance. We may literally say that we sit at the table of fortune, fame, and beauty.

The two Chinamen pulling at the ropes which move the long silken punkahs have an Oriental effect, and this Eastern custom give us always a cool breeze in the dining-room.

The days come and go without event, as usual on shipboard.

At half-past five this morning I am awakened by a tapping on my stateroom door. Now for a dive in the great sea-water tank.

Putting on a Japanese kimono, I repair to the deck, where I find the Captain enjoying a swim. Mounting to the top of the tank, by means of a small ladder, I dive into water fully six feet deep. Can anything be more delightful and exhilarating than this? After a half-hour's swim, I return to my stateroom fully repaid for rising so early.

After meals we generally sit upon the spacious promenade deck, engaged in conversation, cards or other games.

Here are the pretty flying-fish again surrounding us, and rising sometimes many feet above the water.

Off on the horizon, Birds' Island is pointed out to us. As we approach it we can, with the aid of the glasses, see thousands of gulls and other birds resting upon this massive rock. We are now abreast of it. The gigantic rock, bearing no other life than that of the birds which make it their home, and rising several hundred feet out of the water, looks black and dreary. But in the morning, when the sun is rising, and this rugged pile is aglow with the brilliant reflections of a rose-tinted sky, with the glistening colors of the ocean around it, the scene is grandly beautiful. The constant beating of the waves has worn caves at the base of the rock. In many places we can see quite through its foundation.

Saturday, August 8th.—Shortly after breakfast we sail close to Gardiner Rock, an isolated region, uninhabited, unsightly, and desolate.

Our attention has just been drawn to the forward lower deck, where, at the entrance to the hold, the purser and his assistants stand, collecting the tickets of the steerage passengers.

They pass down the hold in single file, handing up their tickets as they go by. The occasion seems to afford them much amusement, judging by their broad smiles and loud laughter.

When they return to the deck they again spread out their small squares of matting, gathered into groups of eight and ten, and settle down to the universal game of "poker," played with dominoes. The Chinese are great gamblers. It is interesting to observe a party of players, earnestly engaged, with a crowd of their countrymen around them, watching their movements. They play all day long, never seeming to tire or lose interest.

The evenings are devoted by the cabin passengers to music, both vocal and instrumental, and playing cards. We are like a large congenial family.

My first lesson in chopsticks is given by a lady who resides in Japan. It is awkward work, and would, I think, be very trying, if one were hungry, to depend upon such a slow means of conveying the food to the mouth. For practice, and to amuse myself, I persevere, and can soon pick up articles of food quite readily. I would not, however, recommend this custom to any one who wishes to enjoy his meals.

I cannot distinguish a living thing upon the great space of water around me. No flying fish, gulls or other birds are visible. All is calm, placid, silent, restful. We have not seen a vessel since leaving Honolulu. I think of the unknown world over which we are sailing, with such apparent ease and safety; of the three thousand seven hundred fathoms (twenty-two thousand two hundred feet) of water, the mountains and deep valleys, the caves, the wondrous vegetable growths and the myriads of living creatures, whose homes are in the sea, all hidden from our sight.

We hope to arrive at Yokohama to-morrow morning at half-past six o'clock and eat our breakfast at the Grand Hotel.

What joy to think of reposing blissfully on land once more, with this monotonous ocean travel, for a time at least, ended.

The sunset is such as to make an artist long to have his sketch block on his knee, and his brush in hand, to perpetuate, if possible, the scene before him.

The sun is low on the horizon, casting in its descent

a brilliant glow over the heavens. The surface of the water responds with crimson light, and for the first time we see the land. The highest point of the great Fujiyama rises to an altitude of more than thirteen thousand feet, against a background of illuminated clouds. As we gaze upon the magnificent scene, the Captain approaches and asks how far we suppose we are from Fuji? Various guesses are made. Some say thirty miles, some fifty. I wishing to overstate, boldly declare the distance to be seventy miles. We are informed that we are one hundred and fifty-seven miles from the mountain. So deceptive are distances at sea. But when one considers the height of Fuji, he ceases to wonder.

This is our last dinner on shipboard, and, according to custom, the "Captain's dinner." Toasts, speeches, and the usual merriment are its accompaniments. After a couple of hours of this entertainment we retire to our staterooms to finish packing. As the night advances, and all is quiet, I sit up in my berth and thrust my head through the port-hole to see what I can of Japan, and whether we are near the coast. Yes, about two miles away lies the land, and now and then I can see lights, but the scene is undistinguishable, and the night dark and chilly. When I step on deck in the morning, I find that we are at anchor in the harbor of Yokohama, and I have my first view of Japan, with the rain coming down in torrents, and everything wet and disagreeable.

There are about a hundred sampans, or shore boats, around the steamer; they are rowed by one or two oarsmen, who, by hideous yells, make known their mission, which is to carry baggage or steerage passengers to the shore. Many accept, at a small cost, rather than wait for the steamer's barge. The hotel launch lies beside

HARBOR OF YOKOHAMA, JAPAN.

the "China," and when we have said farewell to our friends, we step upon it and steam to the wharf.

The hotel porter inquires if we wish jinrikishas to take us to the Grand Hotel? I feel like saying: "Of course! that is what we came to Japan for," but instead, meekly answer "yes." Upon which he calls three from about fifty jinrikishas that are waiting for passengers. Immediately they are before us with their bearers. We take our places in two, the third is filled with our luggage. Off we go at a dog trot, in Indian file.

It is a novel situation! A short ride brings us to the hotel, where the smiling manager informs us that he has awaiting us a fine large room, facing the bay. I wonder at this, having sent him no word. Upon inquiry, we learn that a steamer friend, a resident of Yokohama, has preceded us in his yacht, and engaged the room. And kindness like this is manifested towards us during the whole of our sojourn in Japan. We are met by a good word or deed at every turn.

We proceed to our room, and are preparing for breakfast in the large saloon, when a gentle rap on the door is heard. I open it, and there stands a Chinese tailor, Mr. Ah Sing, with samples of goods in his hands, and asks if we do not want some clothing?

Glancing hastily at his samples I tell him to call again, as we have just arrived, and do not yet know what we will require.

We flatter ourselves upon having easily disposed of this polite merchant, but no sooner is the door closed, than another tap is heard. "Come in!" I cry. "Oh, good morning!" Here stands another tailor, with his arms full of clothing of all styles, and with smiling face solicits our order. We repeat our previous answer and Mr. Chang Chou retires. Then taps and taps. We open to a number of them: Nan Sing, then Aha Sing, and many others. The monotony is broken only by the appearance of a Japanese gentleman. No samples or other wares bedeck his person. I wonder what he can want! Perhaps he is an undertaker, and

THE GRAND HOTEL, YOKOHAMA.

thinks we wish to be buried from the annoyances of the last hour. He is not an undertaker nor a tailor. He is a shoemaker, and politely asks if we do not want some good American shoes? We put him off as we did the others, and at last are ready for breakfast.

Upon returning to our room, and while engaged in

unpacking, we are literally besieged by merchants, tailors, shoemakers, masseurs, guides, and I know not what others, for at last, in desperation, I lock the door, and leave the anxious knockers to imagine that we have died from the pressure of business.

This afternoon we rest. Our room is on the second floor, and before it, runs a wide, well-shaded piazza, facing the beautiful harbor. We entertain ourselves by watching the strange craft in the bay, which are so numerous that many times we expect to see a collision. The men propelling these boats are very scantily clad, wearing only the loin-cloth required by law. They appear muscular and athletic.

On the street are young girls carrying the typical paper umbrella, with babies tied to their backs; men, women, and children, all so odd looking! A living panorama of strange sights!

After dinner, our friend, Mr. C——, knowing that we wish a reliable, honest, and intelligent guide, introduced Mr. Y. F. Shimidzu, a member of the "Kaiyusha Association" of "Licensed Guides of Japan." I like his appearance, and engage him by the month, instructing him to report at the hotel to-morrow. With the repeated bowing incidental to polite Japan, he takes leave.

After dinner we become restless, and think a little peep into the ways of the Japanese at night would be in order. Procuring two jinrikishas, we start off for an hour or two of sight-seeing by ourselves. We can neither speak to our jinrikisha men nor they to us, intelligently, so we arrange, beforehand, that they will take us through some of the business streets, and bring us back to the hotel. What interesting and instructive sights are these, our first glimpses into the real living

RIDE THROUGH THE STREETS OF YOKOHAMA.

Japan! We have read much of this country and its people, but nothing equals the impression made by this ride through the streets of Yokohama by night.

Hundreds of pedestrians throng the streets and sidewalks. Our jinrikisha men whirl rapidly past them, and through the crowds gathered about the hucksters, calling out: "Hi! Hi! Hi!" The groups scatter in all directions, and we leave them gazing after us, queer foreign people.

Stores and booths of every description line the sidewalks, and with the native costumes of buyers and sellers, form a never-to-be-forgotten picture.

As we approach a Japanese theatre, I tap my jinrikisha man with my cane, and motion for him to take us to the entrance and there wait for us.

When we enter we attract much attention, as we are the only foreigners (English or Americans) present. We are given box places, and as there are no chairs, we must sit upon our knees, as is the custom here. Men, women, children and babies compose the audience, many of whom gaze upon us, rather than upon the actors. I do not object to this notice, which would be given to them if the case were reversed, and the citizens of this country were visiting one of our theatres at home. The parquet is a perfectly bare floor, containing neither chairs, benches nor aisles. Here they squat, huddled close together. Where our parquet circle would be, the floor is raised about two feet and enclosed with a railing, within which sit the better classes of the people. During the performance the children walk about the theatre and even across the stage. I see three children, innocent of clothing, playing "tag" upon the stage, while the actors are performing their parts.

The audience present a novel appearance. Children and adults generally wear loose clothing, and frequently only the simple garment called a kimono.

The heat is oppressive, and the air foul from smoking, for in Japan every one smokes, young and old, male and female. Many of the children strip off their garments entirely, and are seen thus, sitting or lying upon the floor. Some of the ladies are so warm that they slip their kimonos off their shoulders, and bare themselves to the waist. Men are quite naked, excepting the loin cloth. In this clad and unclad audience the greatest innocence prevails. No thought of impropriety exists. In their cool attire they seem comfortable and content. Close by us is a pair of lovers, quite young, and the girl very pretty and innocent looking, as she sits there with her kimono dropped to her waist.

Upon returning to the hotel, I engaged the services of a masseur, called in Japan a shampooer, and retire, leaving orders to be called early in the morning. And I may say here, that if an order is given to a Japanese you can be sure that it will be promptly and accurately fulfilled. They never forget, and are as regular as clockwork.

After a warm bath in the morning, I find Mr. Ikeda, the shampooer, awaiting me. He is a good looking young fellow, well built, and of pleasing manners. I observe his proceeding with interest.

He washes his hands with soap and water, then taking from the long baggy sleeve of his kimono a small bag or puff of rice powder, he powders the part to be rubbed, and with gentle manipulations, goes over the whole body, giving the head finally a special and extra rubbing. The entire operation occupies an hour.

THE ENTIRE OPERATION OCCUPIES AN HOUR.

His charge is fifty sen, equivalent in American money to twenty-five cents.

The more common masseurs, both men and women, walk through the streets, blowing at intervals a small wooden whistle, of shrill sound. These shampooers are generally blind, and charge as low as seven sen, or three and a half cents, for an hour's manipulation. The masseur is called Amma, the masseuse, Onna Amma.

This morning is taken up with shopping, until lunch, or "tiffin."

A BLIND MASSEUR OR SHAMPOOER.

Our guide accompanies us everywhere. After tiffin, he calls three jinrikishas for an afternoon ride. The jinrikisha men wear large white canvas hats, on which are stamped in black letters their name, licensed number, and the letters "G. H.," signifying Grand Hotel.

We enter the frail looking carriages, ladies first and the guide in the rear. Our men have also stamped upon their hats their names, which are "Miya," "Cho," and "Suke." We ride in Indian file, two men being employed for each jinrikisha—one in the shafts and one to push at the back. We ride through a very interesting thoroughfare, named Jizosoka Street, where the shops are all open, and we can see the various tradesmen at work. Here are men and women making straw hats and baskets, wooden shoes and sandals. Here are flower girls, cabinet makers, dyers, fishmongers, and dozens of others, all busily engaged in their different occupations, and presenting a scene resembling nothing we have ever before beheld. The total absence of feeling in regard to the exposure of the person, in men, women, and children, is everywhere apparent; women nude to the waist, men wearing nothing but the loin cloth, and children entirely naked, are seen on all sides.

On the way we meet a Japanese funeral procession. A strange sight, compared with our American funerals! The Japanese are much more simple. Two men carry, suspended from the centre of a pole, a closed square box, containing the corpse. This box is called a "kago," and is also used by the Japanese in carrying tourists and other travelers over mountain roads that are too rough for the jinrikisha. Fifteen or twenty mourners following this hearse—some walking, others in jinrikishas.

While descending a very steep hill, I almost have a runaway.

My jinrikisha men are both of light build, and as I

In the Distance is the Beautiful Mississippi Bay.

am somewhat heavy for them, the jinrikisha goes faster and faster down the hill, until it is as much as the men can do to keep the frail vehicle from upsetting. I sit silent, fearing at times that I will be pitched out headlong, but curious to see the wind-up. I do not realize my danger until we have reached the bottom of the

FIRST IMPRESSION OF JAPAN. 131

WE PASS THE SHRINE OF THE GOD, SOSE.

hill, when I thank my stars and the men's good legs for my safe deliverance.

We ride along Izawa Street to the race-course. What an opportunity this part of the country offers to the artist! Upon either side, rice, potatoes, mulberry trees, and many other products cover the fields as far as the eye can see. In the distance is the beautiful Mississippi Bay. We are on a high hill, from which we have a magnificent view of the country around us.

Descending to the plain, we pass the shrine of the god, Sose, whose little wayside temple invites those who wish to worship. We see several persons upon their knees, engaged in prayer.

Bamboo is freely grown here. What a romantic and picturesque landscape is before us. The road is shaded on both sides by bamboo and other tropical trees, and is quite foreign in appearance. Locusts fill the air with their file-like music. The atmosphere is cool and delightful, and the heavens cloudless, their soft blue adding to the beauty of the scene. We come to the little fishing village of Negishi near the bay, which we saw from the top of the hill. It consists of some fifty cottages or shanties huddled together, with heavy thatched roofs, resembling those one sees in the interior of southern Ireland. Plants are grown on the tops of the houses, their roots adding strength to the roofs, and protecting them against the heavy winds that frequently prevail here.

In a short time we arrive at the famous tea house of Tsukimikan (meaning the Moon house), which is situated on the edge of Mississippi Bay. The name of this seashore resort is Honmoku, and here

IN A SHORT TIME WE ARRIVE AT THE FAMOUS TEA HOUSE OF TSUKIMIKAN.

are often seen many bathers frolicking in the cool waters.

Leaving our jinrikishas, the men to rest and refresh themselves with tea and rice, we enter a clean and dainty house, and are met in the doorway by the smiling landlady and about eight little tea girls. These girls are called Kane, meaning coin, but a more polite term is Neisan, little girl. These little tots bow to us profoundly and continually, in accordance with the characteristic custom of this polite nation. No matter on what occasion we meet these interesting people, whether in shops, hotels, or places of amusement, the low and graceful obeisance is never omitted. Of course, our shoes are removed, and we walk in our stockings upon a floor as bright and clean as our table tops at home.

We are invited up-stairs to a room facing the bay, and provided with cushions, upon which we sit à la Japanese, that is upon our knees, or rather on our feet turned under us. We are left alone a short time to rest, after which our guide calls one of the little tea maidens by clapping his hands.

In response one of them cries: "Hei! Hei! Hei!" meaning yes, yes, yes, and in a moment two little cherry faced creatures in Japanese dress come trotting towards us, and go down on their knees with innumerable bows. Being requested to bring some tea, they go out and soon return with a tray holding a pitcher of hot water, a tea pot, tea caddy, and some small cups and saucers. At the same time a wooden box is brought in, containing a bronze bowl filled with hot charcoal. With this, one lights his cigarette. A small bamboo box also appears, to be used as a cuspidor.

After refreshment and a smoke we sit on the veranda in front of our room and watch the bathers. The men, and many of the young girls, wear only the loin cloth. They swim about and have great fun in the water.

As I wish to see a public bath, which I learn is connected with the house, I ask my guide if I can take a hot bath?

He makes the necessary arrangements, and then accompanies me to the first floor, where a private bath is drawn for me. In going to it, I must pass through the public bathroom. Here I see four or five naked men rubbing themselves down. In another corner are seven or eight women, also naked, enjoying a wash. They do not mind my presence in the least. As I pass them, I wonder what a number of Americans would do on a similar occasion. Without doubt a great scramble for secluded places would ensue, if I were compelled to pass them while in this nude state. Not so here. Perfect unconsciousness is manifest, and where no thought of shame exists, purity alone reigns.

JINRIKISHA RIDES AND NOVEL EXPERIENCES.

A Japanese afternoon tea — Shoes in Japan — Yamashita — Mrs. Shimasaki's — The great tattooer — Seeing the "Elephant" — Wooden tickets — Maganechio — Demi-monde — Earthquake — Sitting for our pictures — Along the canal.

OUR guide, ever thinking of some new pleasure for us, suggests a visit to his home, promising us a genuine Japanese afternoon tea. We accept his invitation gladly, and soon after our little wagons stop in front of a two-storied wooden cottage on the outskirts of Yokohama. Taking off our shoes we enter, and are ushered into a room on the second floor. The houses of Japan are generally built of wood, and are not more than two stories high. There is no furniture in the back room, through which we pass, but in the front room we find chairs and tables arranged quite in "American" fashion.

I tell Mr. Shimidzu that I thought we were invited to a Japanese tea. He replies that as it would be uncomfortable for us to sit as the Japanese do, he had chairs and tables introduced into his house for his American and European friends, of whom he has many, for he is considered one of the best and most intelligent guides in Japan. Afternoon teas are called in Japan, "Ocha."

In a short time the two daughters of Mr. Shimidzu, girls of fifteen and sixteen years of age, appear, and are introduced to us in the American fashion. They are very charming. One of them speaks a little English.

Retiring to an adjoining room they give us some music, one playing upon a samisen or guitar. The music is odd and sweet. Then the wife of our guide comes in with smiling face and gracious greeting. What pleasant people these are, ever happy and merry. She sets before us a tray of rice and fried eels, and, instead of knives and forks, chopsticks are handed us. Now I am grateful for my practice on board the steamer, but nevertheless, our awkwardness causes them all much merriment. A small box is placed before us containing incense, or "ko," which, being lighted, fills the room with a sweet, delicate odor. After the rice and eels, a dish of something resembling preserved ginger is passed around. Tea is then served, accompanied by a sweetmeat called "yokan," made of sugar, red beans, and gelatine. We chat as well as we can, with our guide as interpreter. Rare curios, the collection of many years, are shown us. We spend two delightful hours with them, then say good-bye. Having by this time learned the art to perfection, we keep on bowing and bowing until we have reached the threshold, when, with a tip of the hat, which is never seen in Japan, except from foreigners, we betake ourselves to our jinrikishas, and turn our faces homeward.

We wish to become acclimated to this new country by degrees, so think it best to visit places in the neighborhood of Yokohama until our more extensive programme can be carried into effect. Our mornings are devoted to shopping and local amusements.

After "tiffin" to-day, we walk to the canal, where we hire a sampan and are rowed to a bathing resort on Mississippi Bay, about two miles distant. The name of the place is Yamashita, meaning foot of the mountain. Here we find some fifty men, women, and children bathing promiscuously. The beach is lined with tea houses, where persons may watch the bathers and be served with hot tea. There are no bath houses here, where men and women may make their toilets. All changes are made in the open air, "without fear or trembling." There is little to interest us here, so we return to our starting point, pay our boatman, and walk to the noted establishment of Mrs. Shimasaki. A knock at the frail door causes the lady of the house to slide it back, and with courteous bows and smiles to bid us enter. This establishment is devoted to fine embroidery and linen work. We make several purchases, then ask if we may visit the workroom. Upon being conducted thither, we see some nine or ten little girls, so small that really, in walking about, I am afraid that I will accidentally tread upon them. These children are adepts with their fingers and the needle. We are shown a large and delicate piece of work, upon which three of them are engaged at the same time. It represents a cobweb. The design is made by a young man artist, and the girls carry it out with silk and linen threads. It is true to nature, and the portion completed, most exquisitely worked. These girls receive only about five cents a day for their labor.

We also visit the greatest tattooer in Japan, whose name is M. Hori Chiyo. His card bears the following announcement: " Patronized by H. R. H., Princes Albert Victor and George, and having testimony of Marquises, Counts, and other particular families." This circular always accompanies his card: "As my art of tattooing has been frequently noticed in the American and European press. I had a taste of drawing from very young age. I entered the Tokyo Fine Arts Academy, and after graduating in the drawing course, I studied assiduously the art of tattooing. Being not satisfied with the common crude works of the profession, I devised various new methods, and attained to the highest degree of perfection, as to the minuteness and artistic effects, which will delight and surprise to behold. The tattooing being unlike those species of engravings, care must be taken to have the work done in a perfect and high-toned manner; otherwise, once it is executed, cannot be retouched, but remains lifelong on the body as a scar, if badly done and not liked. My specialty is the crest, monogram, and portrait. The distinct minuteness of the work shall not be approached by others. My designs are unlike any patterns kept by others. I make fresh designs every year, and select only those that will suit my patrons, which amounts above two thousand. The needles and materials which I daily employ, I use fresh ones for every patron. I take special precaution against possible dangers, not to use the needles that have been employed for another body. My object is not in making money by the work, but I covet to spread the art all over the world, and promote my reputation. All tourists who come to Japan from Europe and America are solicited to patronize my work, as it may serve as a memento of pleasant sojourn or visit to the fair land of 'Rising Sun' at such and such period of one's age."

We are received by Mr. Chiyo's wife, a bright and pleasant little Japanese woman, who invites us to be seated and excuses herself. In a few moments the world-renowned M. Hori Chiyo enters, and after a cordial greeting, asks us into his workroom. It is our good fortune to see Mr. Chiyo working upon the forearm of a very young man. The design, in many colors, represents the Japanese dragon, and is fully ten inches long. The execution is artistic and exquisite, both in color and detail. I ask the young man, who, by the way, is a Philadelphian, how long he has been in the chair? He replies, since early morning, and that the design will require a day for completion. The designs are selected from a book, containing many hundreds of patterns, and will be produced upon whatever part of the body is desired. Mr. Chiyo assures me that the dyes are permanent, and seems quite alarmed when I tell him that I can remove the design from the body of the gentlemen upon whom he is working. He inquires anxiously how this can be accomplished? I reply: "By cutting off the arm at the elbow." He smiles and looks greatly relieved at what he calls my American wit. His wife's arms, at which he allows me to look, are most beautifully tattooed from the shoulders down. Mr. Chiyo's body is also elaborately decorated, so much so that one could readily imagine that it has a covering of some exquisitely fine fabric. He assures me that he is completely tattooed with his own original designs.

Thinking I have had enough novelty for to-day, I give myself up to an evening on the hotel porch, listening to the Japanese band playing English and American operas. As I am enjoying myself thus, the guide approaches, and with repeated bowing asks if I would like to go out to see the "elephant?" Wondering in what respects the Japanese elephant differs from that in other parts of the world, such as Paris, London, and Berlin, I am, notwithstanding my fatigue, persuaded to go and see him when he is to be seen.

AND THE PEOPLE IN THEIR QUAINT AND PICTURESQUE COSTUMES ARE VERY INTERESTING.

Procuring two jinrikishas, we are soon riding rapidly through the city streets. How beautiful a Japanese city is at night! Thousands of lighted lanterns hang from the shops, and the throngs of people in their quaint and picturesque costumes are very interesting.

We ride along the main street to Onoicho Street, thence to Basha Street, and, crossing the Kanenohashi bridge, we come to Isezakicho, or Theatre Street, which is to me the most interesting street in Yokohama. It seems to be the general thoroughfare. Hundreds and hundreds of men, women, and children promenade the street and sidewalks, laughing, talking, and enjoying life in their own happy way. The stores on either side and the various booths offer their wares at tempting prices to the customer of limited means. For whole squares may be seen merchants who have spread matting upon the street, and placed thereon goods and cheap articles to catch the fancy of the populace. It is not uncommon to see a group of ten, fifteen, or twenty gathered around one of these street venders, who declaims earnestly in praise of his goods, with a joke sandwiched in to hold his listeners until a sale is completed.

In this street theatres and other places of amusement abound, and the excitement is increased by the constant beating of drums and cymbals and the Japanese bands playing national music. Songs and the "samisen" are also heard. Yes, this is the street of all streets in Yokohama!

JINRIKISHA RIDES AND NOVEL EXPERIENCES. 145

At length the jinrikishas halt, and we alight before a Japanese circus. Paying for a ticket to the best part of the house twenty sen, or ten cents in American money, we enter. The tickets of admission are not small cards, such as we use in our theatres, but long wooden tablets, nine and a half inches in length, two inches

WE COME TO ISEZAKICHO, OR THEATRE STREET, THE MOST INTERESTING STREET IN YOKOHAMA.

wide, and a quarter of an inch thick, with Japanese writing on both sides. They are given up at the door as we enter the theatre. Here are also sold wooden shoe checks. For the sum of one sen shoes are checked and left outside the theatre. As I am a foreigner I am allowed to keep mine on my feet. Perhaps they think I wear no stockings, and am ashamed to expose my naked feet.

We are shown to a box on the second floor, from which we view the strange mass of human beings. The performance is poor, compared with those of our great

WE NEXT VISIT THE MAGANECHIO.

Barnum or Forepaugh, the most famous shows in the world. The lower floor is bare of everything save the leather cushions that can be had for one sen, in addition to the admission fee, which is three sen in this part of the house.

Japanese programmes represent the order of the play

by pictures, thus at a glance you are able to follow the performance. Before we leave the circus I ask the guide to purchase for me one of the wooden admission tickets, jestingly remarking that perhaps I can have them introduced into our theatres at home. The ticket agent generously presents me with one of the tablets, for which, however, I return a small fee.

We next visit the Maganechio, entering with our jinrikishas through a lofty gateway. This is one of many places of a similar order throughout Japan. It is a large enclosure, with a moat on one side, and a high stone wall surrounding the houses, which almost form a village of themselves. With the exception of the stores that supply food, clothing, and other articles, the houses are devoted to the demi-monde. There are many streets, with rows of houses, each containing dozens of girls, between the ages of twelve and twenty-four years.

In the front part of each house is a long room facing the street, protected only by a wooden grating, behind which the girls are required to sit in rows, awaiting their selection by a customer. These houses are generally managed by women, and are under the protection and inspection of the government.

Any girl or woman in Japan found guilty of prostitution is arrested and placed in one of these houses of the Maganechio. The government also provides hospitals for these unfortunates.

In justice to many of them, I must state that this life is not always led by them of their own free will. They are frequently placed here by parents to pay off a debt, and are compelled to remain until they have earned a certain sum of money.

Yesterday we had our first experience of an earth-

IN THE FRONT OF EACH HOUSE IS A LONG ROOM PROTECTED ONLY BY A WOODEN GRATING.

quake in Japan. While writing at a table, I was startled by seeing things sway to and fro. The chandelier shook violently, and the building began to rock. For an instant my presence of mind deserted me, but the natural impulse is to run somewhere, and as the doors are generally open, I quickly found myself on the porch with others, awaiting further developments. The hotel continued to sway for nearly a minute, then ceased, and the earthquake was over. But the feeling was decidedly unpleasant. Natives and residents here are quite used to these antics, and look upon an earthquake, unless very severe, as we do upon an April shower. They are of frequent occurrence.

I am told that a prominent scientist stated the islands of Japan are in constant motion, caused by volcanic action, but that the inhabitants have become accustomed to it. Their frail wooden houses, however, readily succumb to a really severe earthquake. It is generally admitted that the safest place during a severe shock is near the house, as many incidents are recorded of natives who have met their death by running into the streets or roads, and been swallowed up by the great seams that opened in the earth.

To-day being clear and cool, we decide to have our photographs taken in Japanese costume; so in the necessary jinrikishas we proceed in Indian file along the Bund, or ocean drive, to the photographer's. On the beach, it being low tide, we see many young girls, in their picturesque costumes, gathering shells, which, we learn, are crushed and used for mortar and fertilizing purposes. Mr. Kimbei, whose studio is situated upon Honcho-Dori Street, is the best photographer in

Yokohama. We enter with our guide, and upon making known our wishes are shown up-stairs to a dressing-room, where a charming little Japanese girl dresses the foreign ladies in Japanese costume. A Japanese gentleman is also engaged to attire the men. This assistance is quite necessary. When dressed, we are told to sit Jap-

HERE MAY BE SEEN THE LANTERN MAKER.

anese fashion, that is, to cross the legs under one; and we remain in this uncomfortable position until our photographs are taken.

When this is accomplished, we ride along the canal to the village of Negishi. It is a very interesting drive on account of the many curious stores that line the

JINRIKISHA RIDES AND NOVEL EXPERIENCES. 151

We Decide to Have Our Photographs Taken in Japanese Costume.

sidewalks. Here may be seen the lantern maker and umbrella manufacturer. Both lanterns and umbrellas are made of oiled paper, and may be exposed to sun and rain without injury. These umbrellas are almost universally used in the country, and to a large extent in the city. Here, too, is the wigmaker, whose custom is

HERE IS A DRAPER DISPLAYING HIS GOODS FROM THE OPEN FRONT.

chiefly among the actors, as the natives generally have magnificent hair. Baldness is almost unknown in Japan. Here is a draper displaying his goods from the open front. In making a purchase, one sits upon a platform in the front of the store, the merchant squatting before you, will show you any article in his stock.

Various street venders offer provisions for sale, carrying, as it were, their stores upon their backs.

On the outskirts of the city we pass a blacksmith's shop, where the men are industriously engaged upon all kinds of iron work, more especially the frames of wagons, jinrikishas, etc.

In the canal is a large barge laden with coal, which is being borne off by men and women coolies in baskets upon their shoulders. As they cross the gang-plank a watchman stands close by with a long, heavy stick to urge them on should they lag in their duty. Boys and girls and some men are knee-deep in the water of the canal, shell gathering. This canal is a very active thoroughfare. Barges laden with vegetables, rice, shells, and various other goods are pushed by men with long bamboo poles or sculled with a large oar.

As we pass through the village we are greeted by the natives with, "O-hayo!" (good-morning), or "Konnichi-wa?" (how do you do?) smiling and nodding their black heads.

At one of the tea houses, where we rest and have tea and sweetmeats, the polite landlady bows so repeatedly and so close to the ground that I entertained fears of her turning a somersault, but her experience in such profound matters enables her to avoid this catastrophe. One cannot help appreciating the kindness and attention universally shown to foreigners;

from both high and low we have found this worthy of note.

At the tea houses throughout Japan, where the tourist pauses to rest a few moments and relieve his cramped limbs after a long ride in the jinrikisha, a small fee of about ten sen is expected for the tea and service. Upon entering one of these wayside inns a small tray, called "bon," is placed before the guest. Upon this is a teapot, teacups, and a caddy of tea, hot water, some sweetmeats, generally mint candy, and a small charcoal fire, from which to light the pipe or cigarette.

KAMAKURA AND ENOSHIMA.

Kamakura—The Icho Tree—Ud-di-jin and Sa-di-jin—Temple of Hachi-man—Onna Ishi and Otoko Ishi—Lotus Pond—Daibutsu—Temple of Kwannon—Katase—Food in Japan—Enoshima—Kin Kiro Inn—Mountain Cave—Goddess of Luck—Diver—Japanese money - Statistics.

WE rise early this morning, the day being favorable for our trip to Kamakura and Enoshima. Kamakura is fifty minutes by railroad, changing cars at Ofuna Junction. The country along this route is full of interest, for many villages are passed, and we see the Japanese in their national costumes and in their low frame houses or huts. Far off in the distance the peak of the noble Fuji-yama is ever in view.

Our guide always accompanies us, but travels second-class, both in the railway coaches and when stopping over-night at the inns. He carries our lunch, which is put up for us at the hotel before we start on a day's jaunt. What strange sights we constantly see at these stations, especially at some distance from the cities! Here are men and women and children in native costume, wearing the proverbial wooden shoes. They may be seen hurrying hither and thither, shuffling their feet and making a noise that sounds as if we had struck a forest at midday filled with locusts.

When we reach the terminus our attentive guide is at the door of our coach, assists us to alight, and calls three jinrikishamen, with their little carriages. Each carriage is provided with an extra man, for our ride from this point is to be a long, hard pull. After a short controversy about the price the guide gives the order, "Go!" and we are off, at a dog-trot gait, for the famous temple of Hachi-man.

On the road we pass through such strange places and see such odd sights that we rub our eyes and wonder if we are not dreaming. Here is a little village; the natives, eager and curious to catch a glimpse of the foreigners, are standing in their doorways, smiling at our strange appearance. Although this road is frequently traveled over by tourists, the interest with which the native looks upon the foreigner never loses its intensity.

The thatched roofs which shelter the cottagers from the sun's rays and the beating storms have become quite familiar to us. We have reached Kamakura. The village is composed of a number of small cottages, shops, and tea houses. Leaving the jinrikishas, we now proceed on foot, passing under two ancient torii (torii meaning literally bird's rest) and over a prettily constructed circular bridge. Beautiful lotus flowers invite us to pause, but we go on, and at last stand on the steps leading to the ancient and renowned temple of

Hachi-man. Midway up we pass under the branches of the noble Icho tree, which is about twenty feet in circumference, and is said to be a thousand years old. It spreads wide its boughs, covered with thick foliage.

LARGE BELL—KAMAKURA.

Still ascending, we see on either side of the wide stairway two wooden images, enclosed in cages and apparently keeping guard over the temple. The one on our right is called Ud-di-jin, or "Right Minister," and that on the left Sa-di-jin, or "Left Minister." These ministers are supposed to keep a safe watch over the temple. Both ministers are covered with paper spit-balls which have been thrown at them from time to time, and have stuck fast. There is a superstition among the Japanese that if a wish be written on paper, then chewed and thrown at a favorite god or goddess, the wish will be fulfilled if the paper adheres to the image; if it falls off it is an unfavorable omen.

We stand before the great temple, within whose walls are enclosed those things which are most sacred to the native of Japan. Curious suits of old armor, masks, swords, and spears may be seen in the series of rooms filled with evidences of ancient history. We pass many shrines, noted in the traditions of this people. Not far from the main temple, enclosed by a wooden railing are two large stones. Upon asking what peculiar interest is attached to them, our guide tells us that the one on the right is called Onna Ishi, or female stone, and the one on the left Otoko Ishi, or the male stone. The peculiar natural formation of the first stone has given it its name. It is of great age. It is said that barren women wishing children may have their generation perpetuated by simply rubbing this stone. The male stone is placed there merely as a companion to the female stone.

Descending the hill, we see at our feet a lovely lotus pond, covering several acres. The leaves of some of the plants are fully four feet in diameter, and the flowers are enormous, measuring from twelve to fourteen inches across. They are white and pink, and are now (August) at the height of their bloom.

We return to our jinrikishas, and a short ride brings us to the presence of the Great Buddha, or Daibutsu, a masterpiece of Japanese art and skill. This image was cast in bronze in 1252 A. D. It is about fifty feet high and ninety-eight feet in circumference; the length of the face is eight feet and a half, of the eyes, four feet, and the ears, six feet and a half. The eyes are said to be of pure gold.

We enter by a gateway into the hollow form of the Daibutsu, and find therein several smaller statues, among them one of Amida-Butsu. Retracing our steps, we stand again before the majestic figure. It is truly a marvelous work, and represents a stupendous amount of labor. A solemn stillness surrounds this idol of the people's faith and hope. As I look up to the calm powerful countenance, I think of the thousands of penitents who annually offer up their prayers to God through this image.

As we stand, filled with wonder and admiration, many worshipers prostrate themselves before the shrine, and with audible prayers supplicate the blessing of the god.

The temple of Kwannon stands upon an eminence overlooking the plain of Kamakura. It is celebrated for the great image of the Goddess of Mercy, which is here concealed from public view behind folding doors. A small fee to the attendant enables one to gaze upon this beautiful idol, which is made of brown lacquered wood, gilded over, and is thirty feet five and a half inches high. There are many small images within the temple, of which much might be said. The god of Money sits upon two sacks of rice, holding in his hand a mallet, and the native belief is that prayer to this god for help in financial affairs will be answered. In front of the shrine is a small wooden image resting on its knees. This god rules that part of the body subject to pain and disease, blindness, deafness, and other afflictions, and if the petitioner will rub the god in a part corresponding with that of the pain in his own body, he will be healed. Unfortunately I have neither aches, pains nor disease, consequently I cannot test the efficacy of this all-powerful idol.

Having seen enough of shrines and temples for to-day, the guide directs our men to the picturesque and beautiful Enoshima. ("Eno" signifies bay, and "shima" island.) But Enoshima is really a peninsula, for it is surrounded by the sea only at high tide. Our ride is along the sea, and we can perceive the village far off at the water's edge. As it is high tide, Enoshima is an island. There is, however, a bridge connecting it with the mainland. As we ride along the beach we see numbers of fishermen, standing up to their armpits in water, fishing with long poles. They are said to be very expert with hook and line, and the fish here are excellent.

At the village of Katase we leave our men, for we must walk from here to Enoshima. We stop and rest at one of the tea houses in the neighborhood, and while our tea is being served we see our jinrikisha men strip off their clothing, consisting of a very light cotton undershirt and a pair of thin trunks, and go thus naked to a tub near by filled with clean water, give themselves a thorough washing and put on fresh suits; then proceed to wash the soiled garments they have taken off, and hang them in the sun to dry. I admire their cleanliness, which may be said to extend to all the inhabitants of Japan. They seem to live more by washing than by eating.

We have had tea and a pleasant rest, and now again, just before leaving, a pretty little girl brings us hot tea and sweetmeats of powdered rice flavored with mint, and the usual charcoal fire, from which we light our cigarettes. Then the landlady bows and bows and bows. Gracious! I think she will never stop! And with every bow she utters the droll words: "Mata-Irasshai" (Please come again). We say, "Sayonara" (Good-bye).

The tea throughout Japan is served very weak, and without sugar or milk. Sugar, butter, and milk are found in this country only in the large cities and open ports. The principal food of the natives is boiled rice, raw eggs, fish raw or cooked, pickles, and saké, a Japanese whiskey distilled from rice.

PASSING THROUGH A TORI WE ENTER THE MAIN STREET.

An hour's walk brings us to the village of Enoshima. Passing through a tori, we enter the main, and, in fact, only street, which is very narrow, with ascending steps and numerous shops, which keep small articles to sell to the tourist, such as boxes, chopsticks, fans, balls made of marble or stone, strings of shells, and pin-cushions.

On the mountain side, facing the ocean, at the end of the street, are three pretty inns which are the favorite resort of the tourist. Many foreigners spend days and even weeks here in summer. I ask the guide to which one we are going. He replies:

"To the best one, the Kin-Kiro Inn."

In a few moments we are at the door. We freely use the words, "O-hayo" (Good-morning), or "Kon-nichi-wa" (How do you do?) and the landlady bows profoundly and repeatedly. Then appear half a dozen pretty little waiting-girls, with sweet smiles, and still more profuse bowing.

We remove our shoes and enter. To-day, at least, I am grateful for this custom, so restful to tired feet. Our tiny maidens precede us to the second floor, where we are given two pleasant rooms facing the ocean. A delightful breeze blows through, directly from the sea.

Our guide prefers to take his meal below, of Japanese food, in his own native fashion. Ours is served in our rooms. A queer little table, about eight inches from the ground, is placed before us, and soft cushions given us to sit upon. I tell them I want to eat with chopsticks, which causes the little maidens much amusement.

We are served with rice, eggs, tea, and sweetmeats, and as we are hungry, the meal is quite palatable. Three pretty girls sit beside us and fan us while we are eating. These girls, sixteen or eighteen years of age, are hired to the inns by their parents, and are generally from the country, many of them never having seen a large town or city. They are called "Chaya Onna," or tea-house women, but I prefer the more polite term of "Neisan," or little girl. Strange are the sights presented by the adjoining rooms! The only partitions are screens, and these are rarely closed in hot weather, so that one is well aware of all that goes on in his neighbor's apartment.

In the room next to us, two Japanese young men are preparing for a dip in the ocean. Having cast off their kimonos, they attire themselves in loin-cloths, and walk by us across the porch and down a footpath to the beach. In another room a mother and her two daughters are also making their toilet for the bath, exchanging their native dress for the kimono provided by the inn for this purpose.

After tiffin, our guide proposes a tour of the island, and we take a long, hot ramble, up and down the hills, with a coolie at our heels carrying our traps. We go through pretty bits of woodland and along a narrow road, bordered by numerous tea houses, and at last reach the open on the other side of the island, at an elevation of six or seven hundred feet.

The cool breeze is refreshing, and we find here several tea houses on a prominent point overhanging the sea;

in one of them we rest and refresh ourselves. We have a magnificent view from this point. The ocean spreads out as far as the eye can see, and from the base of the mountain great rugged rocks project their sharp points along the coast, while the waves come dashing in with a roar, casting their spray high in the air.

We Go Through Pretty Bits of Woodland and Along a Narrow Road.

We descend by steps cut in the rocks, and wander along from point to point, taking care not to slip on the wet stones, until we come to the mouth of a cave in the side of the mountain. This cave has always been considered a sacred spot by the natives. There are many traditions connected with it and the island, the most popular of which is the following:

"In the sixth year of the reign of Kai-Kwa-Tenno, 152 B. C., the site of this cave was the abode of a terrible dragon, who devoured the children of the village of Koshigoe. About that time there was a violent earthquake. Black clouds covered the sea, and the waves mounted to heaven. Celestial music was heard, and in a rift of the clouds appeared the divinely beautiful Benten, the Buddhist Goddess of Luck, accompanied by two lovely boys. The island of Enoshima suddenly rising from the waters, she descended to it, subjugated the dragon, and was worshiped by all the inhabitants along the coast."

Her image, now removed, was placed by Yoritomo in this cave in the year 1182 A. D. The various accounts confuse one as to the actual history of the discovery of the cave. Be that as it may, this is a most picturesque spot. Looking into the cave, you would imagine it to be at least forty feet high. As we enter the waves come rushing with great force to our very feet, as if angry at our intrusion. At a distance of about a hundred and fifty feet we are supplied with candles to illuminate the gloomy depths. The cave becomes smaller and smaller as we advance. Here is a little shrine at which we are expected to make an offering of a few sen for safe deliverance secured by this special god.

The space is now so narrow and low that after going one hundred feet farther, we must stoop to prevent our heads from bumping against the roof. Now we creep through an opening of not more than three feet, and we continue in this cramped position for a distance of apparently about fifty feet, when we are at the end of the cave. How dark, damp, and still it is! Our flickering candles cast about us an uncanny yellow light, and many strange thoughts flit through our brains. What if this spot is really haunted by a powerful goddess, who could appear, and in the twinkling of an eye transport us to some undreamt of realm! I think it wise to offer a prayer to this goddess of luck to get us safely out of this wet and unattractive chamber.

After some twenty minutes more of this meditation, we retrace our steps, and gladly breathe the pure air again with a clear sky above us.

At the entrance to the cave we notice a Japanese athlete standing naked, excepting the loin-cloth about his waist, and poised on the very edge of a huge rock that overhangs the sea. The guide informs us that he is a diver, and for a few sen will plunge to the bottom of the sea, a depth of thirty feet, and, as an evidence of this feat, will bring up shells gathered there. I cheerfully hand the trifling sum required, five sen, for the performance of this hazardous undertaking. Waiting for an enormous wave to reach the edge of the rock on which he stands, the diver plunges into its threatening crest and is lost to sight for fully a minute. Just as I am beginning to feel uneasy, a black spot becomes visible on a breaker that is hissing towards us, and as the wave rushes onward, the speck proves to be the form of the diver. He is literally carried upon its back and landed safely on the rock from which he plunged. He holds in his hand some beautiful shells of mother-of-pearl. As I am relieved of my painful apprehensions by seeing the fellow safe and sound, I double my contribution, which seems to please him immensely.

We walk back to our jinrikishas, and again partake of the hospitality of the polite landlady, and are off for Yokohama, which we reach in good time.

The next few days are spent in resting and making preparations for our tour through northern and western Japan.

In making this journey to the interior, it is necessary to be provided with an extra quantity of clothing, money, flea powder, shoes, towels, soap, and medicine, as such articles are not to be purchased in any but the open port cities.

We leave Yokohama reluctantly, for our reception by both English and American residents has been most cordial, and we have felt very much at home. In traveling in Japan and Hawaii, as well, much of the tourist's pleasure depends upon his letters of introduction, which are absolutely necessary if he wishes to be taken into the social life of the small English and American resident population of these places. In Europe one may travel upon his own merits, but it is not wise to attempt to do so here.

I will here explain the money system of Japan. The values are decimal, with the yen, or silver dollar, as the unit.

One yen contains 100 sen; one sen contains 10 rin. Gold is practically never seen. The silver pieces are: One yen, 50 sen, 20 sen, 10 sen, 5 sen. The nickel piece, 5 sen. Copper pieces: 2 sen, 1 sen, 5 rin, 1 rin. Besides others issued during feudal days, representing: 1½ rin, 8 rin (these are oblong pieces, called tempo, now rarely seen). Paper money is issued to values of 20 sen, 50 sen, 1 yen, 5 yen, and various larger sums.

NOTE.—Japan has a territorial area of 156,000 square miles, comprising 30,000,000 acres of cultivated land, or an amount equal to that of the State of Illinois.

The United States has 3,400,000 square miles, of which 700,000,000 acres are susceptible to the highest state of cultivation.

The total population of Japan in 1892 was 40,718,677 souls. The population of the United States at the last census taken in 1890, was 62,622,250.

Japan is called by the Chinese "Jipango," which, being translated, means the original sun country, or the land of the rising sun, because to them the sun always seems to rise from Japan.

TOKYO AND THE TEMPLES OF NIKKO.

Off for Tokyo—city walls—imperial passport—Atago-yama—en route for Nikko—Cryptomerias—Reiheishi Kaido—Nikko—temples and temples—photographs—great gate—"The Sleeping Cat"—Koshin—wind and thunder devils—sacred stable—red bridge—Inari, Goddess of Rice—Suminohi—Nantai-zan—Daiya-gawa—images of Amida—temple of Jokoji—God of children—to Ashio—Dainichi do—snake garden—pilgrims—Buddhist and Shintoist—Chuzenji—Hannya and Hodo—the Young Prince—Kegon-no-taki.

WE leave Yokohama on the morning of August 25th by train for Tokyo. Rates of travel here are about the same as those in America. There is little worthy of note on this trip of eighteen miles, occupying about fifty minutes. On either side of the road are field after field of rice, with here and there patches of lotus in full bloom. Occasionally we pass a brewery, for the modern Japanese finds that a large majority is demanding the more civilized drink of beer in preference to the ancient and universal saké.

Much of the rice is near perfection and some of it quite ready for the harvest. Rice is planted here, as elsewhere throughout Japan, at different periods, thus there is a certain amount to be cut at various seasons, unlike our American grains, which have but one period for being harvested.

Here are many vineyards and large truck fields, yielding fruit and vegetables. The farms, generally, are irrigated; in many places the water flows naturally from adjacent streams, while at other points it is necessary to dig wells.

In the distance we can see the city of Tokyo, which has a population of 600,000. The low houses of only one and two stories are in strong contrast to New York and Chicago, with their skyscrapers of fifteen and twenty stories.

Arriving at our destination, we take jinrikishas to the "Imperial," a very spacious and imposing stone structure, and one of the best foreign hotels in the place. Here we have pleasant rooms.

A portion of the city is enclosed by a high and massive stone wall, surrounded by a moat. Within this enclosure is the palace of the Mikado, a modern building of semi-foreign architecture. The imperial grounds are entered through open gates guarded by armed sentinels. The Imperial Hotel is also within the enclosure, as well as many shops and residences.

Upon arriving at Tokyo, our first duty after tiffin is to visit the American Minister, Mr. Edwin Dun. Calling at his residence, we learn that he has left the city, and will not return for several days. As we wish to go on to Nikko to-morrow, we ask his affable representative to grant us an "imperial" passport, that is a pass-

TOKYO AND THE TEMPLES OF NIKKO. 173

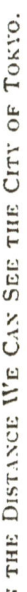

In the Distance We Can See the City of Tokyo.

port that will admit us to every part of Japan without any restrictions whatever. We receive this, together with influential letters, opening to us the doors of many temples and other places generally difficult of access. Now we hold the key that will unlock the barriers that might otherwise obstruct our way.

These imperial passports are not often granted, and only as a personal favor to special friends of the American minister. We were fortunate enough to be pleasantly associated with Mr. Dun on the steamer "China," and he then promised us this passport.

An ordinary passport is issued for tourists in general, extending to certain localities only. Those who wish to go beyond the limits prescribed in this must apply to the minister for additional privileges.

This afternoon we take jinrikishas and ride to the foot of Atago-yama, which resembles many other places of the kind, and has two flights of stone steps leading to the top. One of these, called the men's stairway, is straight and steep, while the woman's stairway is circuitous and less fatiguing. We have a fine view from the hilltop. In the distance we can plainly see Fuji-yama and the city of Tokyo. A small temple, called Atago, is here. Atago is properly the name of a divinity, and the widely spread use of it—for there are Atago-yamas all over Japan—is attributable to the fact that the god especially protects towns against fire.

He is an incarnation of the creatress Izanami and of her last-born child Homusubi, the god of fire, whose birth caused her death. From this point we can see the roof of the imperial palace, with the beautiful woods and gardens surrounding it. This palace has been the residence of his majesty, the Mikado, since 1889. It is said to have cost more than three millions of dollars.

Descending the hill, we enter our jinrikishas, prepared for an hour or two of shopping. A shower comes on, but the leather covering of the jinrikishas and the oil cloth drawn up in front protect us thoroughly. We visit many of the most noted shops of the ivory carver, wood-worker, and bronze-molder, and use the remainder of the day in preparing for our journey to Nikko.

I was startled out of a sound sleep this morning by the blowing of whistles, and jumped up quickly to learn the cause. Had we been suddenly transported to Philadelphia, where the factory whistles blow at seven o'clock every morning? No; we are still in Tokyo, and the hour is six in the morning, when the steam whistles blow to notify the workmen that it is time to begin their daily labors.

We take an early train for Nikko, a distance of ninety-one miles, or thereabout, which we expect to accomplish in five and one-half or six hours. Our route is not very interesting. The farms on either side of the railroad are well cultivated, the chief product being rice. Much truck is raised, such as sweet potatoes, beans, and lettuce. All these fields are irrigated from rivers and streams close by. The fields are not separated by fences or hedges, the only distinction being the difference in vegetation. As we approach the village of

THE VILLAGE OF HACHI-ISHI.

Hachi-Ishi we see a beautiful road, bordered on either side by lofty and majestic cryptomerias. This picturesque highway runs parallel with the railroad for fully ten miles. It is called Reiheishi Kaido (kaido signifies highway). It is so called because in olden times the Reiheishi, or Envoy of the Mikado, used to travel along it, bearing gifts from his imperial master to be offered at the Mausoleum of Ieyasu.

At last we reach Nikko. What a scene of beauty and grandeur is before us! A popular Japanese proverb says, "Nikko wo minai uchi wa, 'kekko' to iu na!" ("Do not use the word 'magnificent' until you have seen Nikko.") Here nature and art combine to form one of the most wonderful places on the earth. Mountains, cascades, monumental forest trees have always been here. In the seventeenth century, to these were added the mausolea of the illustrious Shogun Ieyasu, founder of the Tokugawa dynasty, and of his scarcely less famous grandson, Iemitsu.

We are surrounded by stately mountains, the greatest of which, the noted Nantai-zan, towers high above its neighbors. Taking jinrikishas, we proceed to the Nikko hotel, a mile and one-half from the station. By this time we are quite accustomed to the Japanese carriage. Though at first one is apt to pity the poor men in their labor of drawing him up and down the hills, in this age of travel, one's nerves and feelings soon become hardened. Reaching the hotel upon the mountain side, some two thousand feet above sea level, we learn, to our disappointment, that it is filled to overflowing.

Nikko is the popular resort of foreigners residing in Yokohama, Tokyo, and the other large cities. It is said that earthquakes, so frequent in Japan, do not occur in this region. It is noted as the mart for such skins as the badger, deer, marten, wild boar, etc., from which slippers and other articles of European wear are manufactured. Various dishes, cups, trays, and curios are also found here, made of jindaiboku, a fossil wood, brought hither from Sendai. After many gesticulations, much talk, and a vast amount of patience, the latter a very necessary virtue in Japan, we are accommodated with rooms, and, being tired, we bundle off to bed after a semi-foreign dinner, hardly realizing that at last we have arrived at one of the most famous resorts in all Japan. We rise bright and early, rested, and ready to "do" Nikko.

The very thought of visiting all the innumerable temples and shrines of this part of Japan is enough to exhaust one's brain at the outset. Yes, the temples are inexhaustible! We must see "some" of them; and after a leisurely survey of the situation we will select only the masterpieces of ancient Japanese art. We devote two days to the temples, and I cannot begin to tell you what two days of sight-seeing in the temples means. The beauty of architecture and construction, the carving, the gold, silver, and bronze ornaments, the decorations, all dazzle the eyes, and the brain is wearied by the multiplicity of grandeur. Most of these temples are surrounded by the sacred cryptomerias. Pilgrims and travelers come from far and near to behold the great works of their ancestors, and offer prayers to the various gods. I have already taken many photographs within the sacred enclosures, and am still at work, when a man rushes breathlessly up to me, declaring that I am doing a sacrilegious thing. I instantly put my camera in its

! Most of These Temples are Surrounded by the Cryptomerias.

case, and am walking away, when he intimates that I may continue my work if I will pay for the privilege. As I have taken all the pictures I desire, I decline his offer.

I will mention a few of the interesting sights among the famous temples of Nikko. The "Great Gate" is filled with elaborate carvings of various birds and animals. The elegance of this gate is in keeping with the grandeur of the temples. The interior of the Iyeyasu temple is of superb splendor, even the ceilings being elaborately decorated. The same may be said of the Iyemitsu temple, the gorgeousness of whose surround-

THIS GROUP REPRESENTS THE BLIND, DEAF, AND DUMB MONKEYS.

ings can be appreciated only by a visit in person. The carving on many of the doors is marvelous.

Ascending several flights of stone steps we approach the mausoleum of the ancient founder. Over one of the gates may be seen the famous carving in wood of "The Sleeping Cat," the most celebrated work of Hidari

Gingoro, also a well executed group of monkeys, called Koshin. This group represents a blind monkey, a deaf monkey, and a dumb monkey, and is symbolic of the Japanese principle, never to see, hear, or speak evil of

WIND DEVIL.

any one. Throughout Japan you will everywhere see slabs of stone and wood with this group of monkeys in relief upon them.

Upon either side of the gateway are wooden images of the "Wind Devil," which is supposed to rule the winds, and the "Thunder Devil," who controls the storms.

These images, called Mio, are placed here to guard the sacred temple. We visit also the stable in which is the sacred white pony, kept for the use of the god. The workmanship of this bronze portal is of wonderful beauty. Here we have a fine concentrated view of this whole group of temples, and the splendor of this consecrated spot.

A short walk from the temple brings us to the Red Bridge, or Mi Hashi, which is worthy of note. It spans the Daiya gawa, and may be viewed from another and public bridge, a few feet lower down the stream. From this last we look upon the scene before us in wonder and admiration.

In the background are lofty mountains clad in verdure, towering thousands of feet heavenward, while at their base the beautiful waters of the Daiya gawa flow in rapid and tempestuous course. In the foreground is the Mi Hashi, the sacred bridge, formerly closed to all persons but the Shogun, excepting twice a year, when it was opened to pilgrims. It stands upon a spot where, according to legend, the saint Shodo Shonin crossed the stream on a holy mission. It is about eighty-four feet long and eighteen feet wide, and was built A. D. 1638. Its gates are closed and securely locked.

We take many beautiful trips over the mountains and into the neighboring villages, and are

THUNDER DEVIL.

never weary of this unlimited pleasure-ground of the tourist.

We take over and over again the picturesque ride to

Hachi Ishi. In this ride we pass a little temple standing aside from the road, and dedicated to Inari, the goddess of rice. The figure of a fox, which is always found in the temples of Inari, is not, as some suppose, a tribute to the fear inspired by that wily beast. Inari is the fox deity.

In this temple, screened from public view, are many large and small images of the sexual organ of man, some weighing about three hundred pounds. I learn that these images, formerly worshiped by the natives, were removed from their temple some ten years ago by an edict of the government.

A heavy rain, a frequent occurrence in these mountains, keeps us prisoners in the hotel. This "rain rest" is a welcome event to the tourist, giving him not only the needed repose for body and brain, but also time for letter-writing and repairs.

To-day is chilly and unpleasant, as neither stoves nor furnaces are known in Japan, outside the large cities, and travelers, when cold, must resort to extra clothing. There is, it is true, a wooden box filled with ashes, upon which red-hot charcoal is laid. These fires are called Hibashi or Suminohi, meaning charcoal fire. They are common throughout Japan, being the only means of affording heat to the houshold. During the cold weather a native will frequently wear four or five kimonos at one time.

The rainy days are also useful in planning trips. We are attentively studying our maps with reference to a journey to the interior of this country.

After a good rest we start out with renewed strength for a little more sightseeing. The day being fair, our guide has forestalled all discussions as to plans by se-

THE GREAT GATE.

curing jinrikishas for a little tour to some neighboring places.

A half-hour's ride brings us to a little tea house, where we stop for rest and refreshments, sitting on the floor, as is the custom. The great Nantai-zan (zan, mountain) rising to a height of eight thousand one hundred and fifty feet, is on our right, some distance away. What a gloriously beautiful mountain! The clouds clustering about its lofty peaks partly hide them from view. The purple and blue tints that color its giant form, with the more delicate shades of green at its base, render it a study for the palette of the skilful artist. On our left is the Nikko range, also clothed in varied hues. At our feet is the Gamman-ga-fuchi, one of many pools that may be seen in the Daiya gawa. How the waters seethe and boil, washing continually the huge boulders that line the banks on either side. As we descend these banks we are obliged to use great care lest we slip on the wet moss-covered rocks and be carried away by the rushing torrent, now swollen by heavy rains.

There are many idols and images with historic records in the various niches of the rocks. On the opposite bank a hundred small figures placed in a row are called the "Images of Amida."

As we look at them we feel that ancestry is scanning us, and a hundred voices greeting us with the words, "O-hayo," as we pass by. Once more we are in our jinrikishas, still following the road that skirts the pretty Daiya gawa. This stream has its source in Lake Chuzenji, upon the Nantai-zan.

Now we turn our faces homeward, stopping, however, at the Temple of Jokoji, which is near the hotel.

Passing through a gate of exquisite beauty, we enter the sacred grounds, which seem to have been used as a cemetery, for hundreds of tombstones are erected here; they are of every shape, and present a strange appearance. Many stone lanterns stand within the enclosure, memorials of priests and other celebrities who once

INTERIOR OF IYEMITSU TEMPLE.

lived on the earth, but have now taken their places in the Celestial world. A stone image, fully six feet high, attracts our attention. This is Koyasu-Jizo, the god of children. His image is covered with pieces of red and white linen of all sizes. It is said that mothers of newly-born babes bring these offerings and tie them on the idol, that he may care for their children and protect them from sickness all their lives. Or, if children are sick, a strip of cloth is suspended from the image by the mother, with prayers that they may be healed.

KOYASU-JIZO, THE GOD OF CHILDREN.

To-day we go to Lake Chuzenji. Breakfast is over, and at 8.30 our guide is at the door with jinrikishas and three men to each wagon. That means that the journey is to be a hard one. The sky is clear and the air cool, and with fleet-footed men we go at a good pace. Our road is along the bank of the Daiya gawa, and is the highway between Nikko and Ashio. After riding a short distance we reach the Dainechi-do, which means the temple of the sun goddess. Here we alight and enter a pretty garden, taking some refreshment at the tea house within. This garden is well worth a visit, not only the perfect type of a beautiful Japanese garden, but also on account of a large spring which oozes out of the earth and forms a lake. The water is pure and cool, coming directly from the mountain beyond. In the centre of the spring a small stone image is supported by stone slabs. This is Ugagin, or the Snake Garden.

Yesterday we saw the Prince, son of the Mikado and heir to the throne of Japan, resting in this garden, surrounded by a staff of officers. He is a lad of seventeen, rather prepossessing in appearance. We learn that he is making a minute tour of his native country. At many places along the route we see evidences of his visits in extra decorations and arches of green.

As we continue, we find the road rough and stony. Our frail carriages are pitched to and fro, and it is a mystery how we are carried for miles along such paths without a breakdown. On the way we see caravans of horses, heavily laden with all kinds of merchandise, and led by a man or woman, it is hard to tell which; the dress is precisely the same, only the women often wear some kind of white linen head-gear. We pass many women and small girls, carrying great wicker baskets filled with green grass. Some of them are so small that they bend almost double beneath their heavy burdens.

AS WE CONTINUE WE FIND THE ROAD ROUGH AND STONY.

At various times we see groups of four or five women dressed in peculiar costumes. These are pilgrims on the way to the temples in and about Nikko. These devotees will walk miles at certain times in the year, to worship at some particular shrine of Shinto, or temple of Buddha. Although the Shinto religion is indigenous to Japan, there are here many followers of Buddha. It is not uncommon for one to be born a Shintoist, and die a Buddhist.

Here comes a curious looking man. He carries a tray upon his head, containing cakes and pies, and calls out his wares in a loud voice as he goes along.

NOW THE SCENERY BECOMES STILL MORE BEAUTIFUL.

Our little human horses run briskly, crying out: "Hi! Hi! Hi!" to any carts or persons that obstruct the way, and we, interested in our experiences, heed little the bumps and joltings that now and then fall to our lot.

We now come to a fork in the road, called Futamiya.

The main road leads to Ashio, while the path to the right goes to Chuzenji, and this latter one we take. Our way is still bounded by the stream whose pure waters come from Lake Chuzenji. Now the scenery becomes still more beautiful, woods and mountains completely surrounding us, while the picturesque stream, in its tempestuous flow, beats against the thousands of boulders of all sizes that lie in its path, at times throwing its spray high in the air. Thus we have a beautiful accompaniment to our journey.

The path grows narrower as we penetrate the cañon, sometimes barely allowing a passage for the jinrikishas. On one side is the stream, ten or fifteen feet below us, on the other towers the mountain, several hundred feet above us, a solid wall of granite. Occasionally a small bridle stream winds its way down the mountain side. We are gradually ascending, step by step. As Lake Chuzenji lies at an altitude of four thousand three hundred and seventy-five feet, and Nikko is two thousand feet above sea level, we must climb two thousand three hundred and seventy-five feet before we can look upon this body of water.

At last we reach the hamlet of Uma-gaeshi, meaning literally "horse-send-back." Our guide tells me that formerly ascent to the lake was made on horseback, and this hamlet takes its name from the fact that at this point the horses were sent back. Here we stop at one of the many tea houses, where we have some good hot tea, and finish off with a bottle of "Japanese" brewed beer. Our faithful men also enjoy their rest, and rice and tea.

From this point the ascent is steep and difficult. My guide tells me that men are rarely or never carried up the mountain from this point; that only the ladies remain in the jinrikishas. At this I take off my coat and vest, and rolling up my sleeves and trousers, prepare, with a stout staff, to climb by steep and short cuts, through the thick brush and undergrowth, while the ladies sit in the jinrikishas, and are pushed and hauled up by five men to each wagon. The path is wet, muddy, and unpleasant, barely wide enough to walk, and at times so slippery that I seat myself unexpectedly in its uninviting arms, much to the detriment of my trousers and appearance generally. However, I comfort myself with the thought that the road to all good things is a hard one, and push on and on, sure of being amply rewarded in the end. By this time, what with the heat of the day and my great exertions, I am perspiring profusely.

While resting at the hamlet, we saw several Japanese ladies descending from the lake by means of the yama kago, a small chair suspended from a pole carried by two coolies. The term yama kago means literally "mountain chair."

As we climb, we can see the road winding away below us. Now we rest at the Missawa tea house. From this point the scene is wilder and more picturesque. Again we plunge into the dense undergrowth of the woods, following a narrow path.

Another opening, where there are several tea houses.

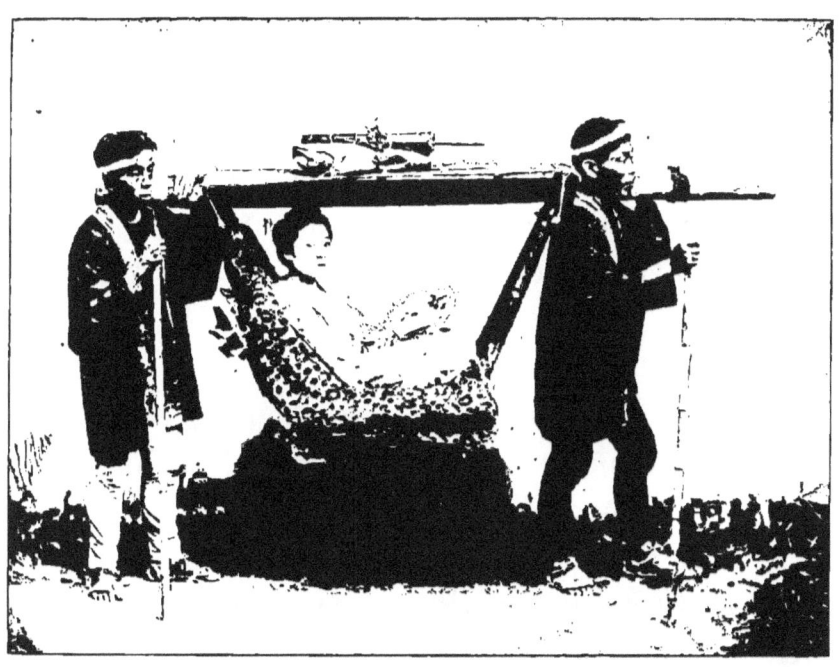

WE SAW SEVERAL JAPANESE LADIES DESCENDING FROM THE LAKE BY MEANS OF THE YAMA KAGO.

What a magnificent view! Far down in the cañon can be seen scattered tea houses, looking like children's toys, while before us rise lofty summits, clothed in green. At some distance on the left, a beautiful waterfall may be seen rushing forth from a deep crevice in the mountain, full seventy feet in height. This fall is named "Hannya," while on the right, not far from its companion, is a smaller stream, falling to a great depth below. This cascade is called "Hodo."

We rest a half-hour, and take some refreshment, then continue the ascent. This part is rougher and more arduous than any previous experience. At last we are rewarded by seeing Chuzenji Mountain at our feet, for we have really reached the summit. Joining the rest of the party, we ride a short distance to the lake. A number of cottages are situated upon its shore, for this is a summer resort for many English and American families.

We go to the best Japanese inn for tiffin. This inn is named Komeva, meaning "rice house." Engaging a room, our guide requests the landlord to furnish us with a table and chairs. Soon the luncheon is on the table. Knives, forks, spoons, and dishes are provided, and we eat tiffin in American style, our guide, as usual, preferring his chopsticks in an adjoining room.

After tiffin, we view the lake and enjoy the scene before us, then visit some noted shrines and temples in the neighborhood. On our way we observe clean sand strewed along the paths and green arches erected here and there, and upon asking the reason of this, are informed that the young prince visited the place yesterday, and this is the custom whenever he appears.

We walk to the temple of Futare-san (name of God), also to a number of other interesting spots, then returning to the jinrikishas ride to the Kegon-no-taki waterfall. This is a magnificent spectacle. The great volume of water dashes wildly over a lofty precipice into an enormous basin, walled in with rocks two hundred and

LAKE CHUZENJI.

fifty feet below. Descending the mountain side, we stand upon a projecting rock, from which we have a closer view of the falls and realize its extent and the force with which it precipitates itself into the whirlpool.

Once more in the jinrikishas we begin our homeward

journey, the descent in many places being so steep that we are compelled to get out and walk.

The beauty of the scenes around us cannot be described by pen or pencil! Only he who has seen them can feel the thrill here experienced in the presence of some of the most sublime and wonderful of nature's handiworks.

We reach the hotel in time for a good hot dinner, to which we do ample justice.

IN THE HEART OF JAPAN.

A journey to the interior—Outfit—At the station—Country people—Omiya—Second-class car—Silk-growing district—Annaka—Asama-yama—Iwafune-san—Miyozi-san—Yokogawa—Usui Pass—Tunnels—Karuisawa—Making a bed—A bath—Iwamurata—Chikuma-gawa—Nagano Zenkoji—Inarimura-Shimohigano—Bowing - Tanbajegma—Saigawa—Japanese artists—A feast—Silk-weaving mill—Presents—Night watchmen.

To-day, Sunday, we make final preparations for a tour through Central Japan, which will last several weeks. Maps and guide-books have been studied and the route carefully planned. We intend going by rail from Nikko to Omiya, Mae-bashi, Karui-sawa, Nagano, thence to Naoetsu, the terminus of the railroad. By jinrikisha and on foot we proceed to Niigata, and, if wind and weather are favorable, we will visit the island of Sado, which can be reached by a small steamer from the mainland in about five hours. This island is noted for its gold and silver mines.

From Niigata, still by jinrikisha and on foot, over the mountain passes, we will go to Sendai, where we again take the railroad to Morioka and Aomori, then return to Nikko.

My guide assures me that this trip will embrace beautiful scenery, a strange country, and costumes and customs quite out of the ordinary line of foreign travel. My object in this journey is to go far away from the beaten tracks, and see how the real Japanese live at home, untainted and unaffected by the progress of civilization. I learn that recent floods have extended over this section of the country, also that disease has visited some of these districts—facts which may interfere to some extent with my plans, but we shall endeavor to carry them out as faithfully as possible.

Our outfit would bring a smile to the face of the modern traveler, including, as it does, kimonos, shoes, and various articles of clothing, medicine chest, candles, tobacco, flea powder, cameras, and painting materials, as well as provisions, cooking utensils, dishes, and knives and forks, all of which are necessary on leaving the larger cities.

The day of starting is a fine one. The sun shines down in all his glory, and it is a superb morning, even for "The Land of the Rising Sun." Up at 5.30, and warmly dressed, after breakfast I find the guide awaiting me with smiling face and his morning greeting, "O-hayo." The jinrikishas are ready, and soon we are on our way to the village of Hachi-Ishi, commonly known as Nikko. Arriving at the station, we find a number of natives, with here and there a foreigner, awaiting the opening of the gates that admit one to the train. This crowd of travelers is very interesting to me, while I seem to be just as curious an object to them. The gates open and the cars are filled with the motley throng. The bell rings, the whistle blows, and at 7.45 we are off for the heart of Japan. As we steam southward to Ut-so-no-miya we again pass the beautiful avenue of cryptomerias.

Many odd sights meet our eyes as we ride through the country. Now and then a horse laden with bags, baskets, and odds and ends, always led by a man or woman, moves along the road. The clothing worn by these people is loose and open: a straw hat, a pair of sandals, and in many cases a piece of matting about three feet square, tied loosely over the shoulders to protect them from the rain or excessive heat of the sun.

I observe gates at many points where the railway intersects the road. These gates are almost invariably managed by young Japanese girls. On the road to Omiya we cross the Tone-gawa, by a strong, well-constructed bridge. Having forty minutes at Omiya, while waiting to make connection, I stroll through the place, but see nothing of interest but the great Fuji-yama in the distance, extending its lofty head far into the clouds. How noble and grand it looks!

On leaving the station we can plainly see Fuji-yama on our left and the Nikko range on our right, having described a somewhat circuitous path in our journey thus far. Our train goes speeding (!) on at the rate of fifteen miles an hour. The cars in Japan do not appear with such encouraging legends as those in America, such as "The Flyer," "Lightning Express," "Wild Cat," and similar high-sounding titles. We are in a second-class car. This is not only a cheaper mode of travel, but when there are no ladies in the party the comfort is almost equal to that of first-class compartments. In our section are several Japanese, among them a young girl of about twenty years, evidently alone. Next to her sits an old man, dressed in a kimono, a felt hat and wooden shoes. The day being hot, the man cools himself by lifting his kimono up to his waist and fanning his bare legs with it, regardless of a lady's presence or ourselves.

The houses we pass are built of wood, with here and there one of stone. The roofs are made of shingles, heavy tiles or thatch. As far as Isobe the fields abound in silk mulberry and rice. I learn that the country between Omiya and Isobe is the great silk-producing district. The valued food of the silk worm is obtained by planting a small branch from the parent mulberry tree, and this, when rooted and grown into full leafage, is cut or plucked from the ground and placed in a large basket for the worms to feed upon, or the leaves are stripped from the branches and put in the basket. In this section are large factories, where the silk is spun from the cocoons.

It is interesting to watch the men, women, and children cutting and gathering in the rice. A sickle is used for cutting the rice straw, a slow and tedious operation. A cluster of rice is held in the hand, and thus cut, the bunch being carefully laid down, to be gathered by the following laborer. For threshing, a stand is

It is interesting to watch the men, women, and children cutting the rice.

used, with a steel blade, three inches long and six wide, with teeth on one edge. A cloth is placed on the ground under the blade to catch the falling rice, as a handful of the rice straw is drawn through the steel teeth.

The rice is hulled in an odd and ancient manner. A

certain quantity is put in a stone basin, and a heavy weight, raised by a lever, is let fall into the basin. The process is slow, but as time is no object in Japan, these primitive ways have no drawbacks.

The costumes of the people in these districts are odd and various. Many coolies walk along the roads in

THE RICE IS HULLED IN AN ODD AND ANCIENT MANNER.

their large straw hats and coats. The country peasant sits by the roadside with his load of merchandise, resting and smoking his small pipe.

We have a fine view from the car window at An-naka station. Here we behold mountains on all sides. The lofty and picturesque Asama-yama rises to a height of

IN THE HEART OF JAPAN.

eight thousand five hundred feet above the sea. Here, too, is Iwa-fune-san (Iwa, rock, fune, boat, and san, mountain), named from the shape of its peaks, which are like a huge boat, from stem to stern. In the distance, on our right is Ikao mountain, not least in this region, where all is interesting and beautiful. Nearer

MIYOGI-SAN WITH POINTED CLIFFS GREAT ARCHES AND SEEMING CASTLES.

may be seen Miyogi-san, or "rocky mountain," rugged and picturesque, with pointed cliffs, great arches, and seeming castles that inspire one with a longing for the artist's brush and the poet's pen to carry these wonderful scenes to all the countries in the world.

At Yokogawa we stop about twenty minutes, when I

leave the car to stretch my cramped limbs and bathe my face and hands at a neighboring fountain. I am immediately surrounded by a dozen children, who are much amused at my strange appearance. I say to them, "Komban-wa" (Good evening), which is received by a burst of laughter.

Our train consists of eight passenger coaches and two very powerful locomotives, one forward, and one at the rear end of the train, for we are to be pushed up an incline of one foot to fifteen, over the Usui Pass, from Yokogawa to Karuisawa station. In this short ride we pass through twenty-six tunnels, whose total length is two and three-quarters miles, the longest one extending one thousand seven hundred and seventy-two feet.

For safety the engines run upon a sort of cogged chain, placed between the rails; for if a brake should slip, or an accident happen, we would all be hurled to the bottom of the incline.

Some of the tunnels are quite short. They are all built of brick or stone. We pass through one after another until we reach Karuisawa at last, at an elevation of four thousand feet. Here we spend the night. The air is cool and pleasant, and after a short walk we arrive at a real Japanese country inn. This is my first experience of "board and lodgings." I engage a room adjoining my own for my guide, who at once begins to prepare for supper, unpacking knives, forks, and dishes.

I make out finely with canned meats and some preserves, added to the customary rice and tea, and enjoy a good meal with a ravenous appetite.

As the evening advances, and I have finished writing up my journal and studying the guide-book, the guide calls a Neisan, and directs her to make my bed

A JAPANESE BED.

You must know that away from the cities, both in inns and private houses, the rooms are wholly unfurnished. Only in places frequented by foreigners are tables, chairs, or stools to be found. The bed is made in this fashion: First of all, flea powder is sprinkled abundantly over the straw mat which covers the floor. Upon this a four-inch mattress is laid; sheets are spread over the mattress and two or three down quilts, and when the mosquito netting is hung over it and an oil-lighted paper lantern placed beside it, you have the genuine Japanese bed. My first experience of this floor bed is not satisfactory. I have a constant fear of rats, mice, centipedes, roaches, and other vermin. But I sleep the sleep of the fatigued, and do not waken until six o'clock in the morning.

I tell the guide that I wish to take a bath, not in the general tub, with other men and women, but by myself. In a few minutes I am informed that the bath is ready. Where is it? What is it? A large tub is placed on the narrow porch in front of my room, exposed to all the rooms that face this part of the inn. It is filled with hot water, and I am expected to undress and wash here! Thinking it best to adapt myself to this primitive custom, I finally undress and begin my bath, concealing myself as best I can behind a towel. It is a very embarrassing position. However, I am clean and refreshed by my trying bath, and I feel that I have the best of it. The jolly landlady has given me the best room in the house. The cost of this room overnight, with charcoal fire, lamp, and bath, is one yen, or fifty cents. I charm the landlady and Neisan, who surround me, by conjurer's tricks and similar entertainments for an hour, then with an "Arrigata" (thank you) and " Sayonara " (good-bye), we pick up our traps and are off by train for Nagano.

This part of the journey is very interesting. A descent of nearly four thousand feet causes the little train to move more rapidly than usual, and the road is considered the most picturesque in Japan. There are deep gullies in the mountain sides, down which flow streams of water to the rivers below. On either side of the railroad the golden harvest of the rice field is ready for the reaper. Only a short distance away the Asama-yama rises in all its glory. The day is clear, and the mountains, as they come into view one after the other, present a magnificent panorama to my enraptured gaze.

From Oiwake, where the Nakesendo, or old mountain road, is left behind, and thence to Komoro, we have the plain of Iwamurata, with Yatsu-ga-taki and Asama-yama in the background.

With what interest I gaze upon this scene, and how I long to rest here and paint these gorgeous pictures! But I dare not pause, for the journey before us will not admit of delay here, so I can only store them away as mental pictures that will brighten many a future day.

I shall never forget the flood of light cast by the sun upon these mountains and the valley below, the dark green of the pines contrasting with the lime and lava on the mountain side.

From Komoro to Neda the road runs through the valley of Chiku-ma-gawa, whose southern bank consists of a series of bold bluffs.

We have a full view of the Shinshi-Hida, massive and grand, and after crossing the Chikuma-gawa and the Saigawa we arrive safely at Nagano, and take jinrikishas to the Fuji-ya Hotel, called in Japan Taikiokukwan. My guide engages for me the only foreign or American room in the place. I find it clean and pleasant, with a fine view of the mountains and plains. It contains an iron bed, some chairs, and a table, after the American fashion. This room is looked upon by the natives as a queer place, but one possessing all the comforts of an American home.

After tiffin I walk about the town with my guide, and am much embarrassed by the stares of those whom we meet, some of the people even standing still to watch us pass. At times a dozen or more of them are at our backs, laughing at my speech and dress.

If any one thinks, sitting in his easy-chair at home, that the Japanese are familiar with our ways and costumes, let him follow in my footsteps and he will soon lose this impression.

We visit the temple of Zenkoji, one of the most celebrated in the whole empire. It is dedicated to Amida and his two followers, Kwannon and Daiseishi, a group of whose images is here enshrined.

"This sacred group is said to have been made by Shaka Muni out of gold found on Mount Shumi, the centre of the universe. After various vicissitudes in China and Corea it was brought to Japan in 552 A. D. as a present from the King of Corea to the Mikado on the introduction of Buddhism into Japan. All the efforts of the Japanese enemies of Buddhism to make away with the image were in vain. Thrown into rivers, hacked at, burned, it survived all, and finally found a resting-place at Zenkoji or Nagano in 602 A. D."

The main temple, erected in 1701 A. D., is a building of two stories, one hundred and ninety-eight feet in depth, and one hundred and eight feet in breadth, with a huge gabled roof, which is supported by one hundred and thirty-six pillars, and contains, it is said, sixty-nine thousand three hundred and eighty-four rafters, the same number as the written characters contained in the Chinese version of the Buddhist Scriptures. A space of eighty-eight mats, one thousand six hundred square feet, is set apart for the worshipers, many of whom we see upon their knees, praying to the various gods. There are many old relics in the recesses, also some mementoes of the recent Chinese Japanese war, such as swords, spears, guns, and armor plate. The images in every available spot, and the silent devotees absorbed in prayer, render the scene solemn and impressive. We are followed by a large crowd, as we inspect the different features of this old temple. When we are outside, I perceive some workmen repairing the roof. The shingles used are strips of wood fifteen inches long

MANY PILGRIMS ARE HERE IN THEIR ODD COSTUMES.

and four inches wide. Upon each strip is painted the name of a person who contributes to the maintenance of the temple. The names of all subscribers, whether the contribution be large or small, are thus painted upon single shingles, which are used in repairing the roof, in this manner perpetuating the generosity of the donor. Many pilgrims are here in their odd costumes, and are seen at every village and highway along the route, generally ringing a bell, or striking a gong, or obtaining a meagre living by begging from door to door.

One wonders at first why so many shrines and temples are seen throughout Japan, but when he learns that to every city, town, and village belongs at least one shrine and one temple, his wonder ceases. I am also informed that every Japanese home contains a Buddha and a Shinto god. The Shinto gods are the idols of their every-day life, but the Buddha is the God to whom the spirit in man takes its flight when death comes. The Shinto shrine is distinguished from the Buddha temple by always having a torii placed before it.

It is the fashion, in the interior of Japan, for the women to blacken their teeth—an ugly and unbecoming custom.

I experience much comfort in my American room, although there can be no comparison between it and the mode of living it is supposed to represent. To-day I gain much information in regard to the production and weaving of silk, and enjoy the society of several very interesting Japanese gentlemen.

Last evening my guide received a call from a gentleman cousin and a pretty young niece, who gave us both a warm invitation to visit their home in a village some distance away. This village is also the birthplace of my guide. This is an opportunity for which I have longed. The people are educated country people, in

WE PASS GROUPS OF CHILDREN WHO STARE AT ME.

comfortable circumstances. When they bade us farewell, they presented me with a handsome box of bonbons, exquisitely wrapped, with the daintiness for which this nation is so celebrated. I am informed that this custom of presenting gifts to strangers is quite common.

To-day, therefore, our destination is the village of Inarimura-Shimohigano, four miles from Nagano. At nine o'clock our jinrikishas are ready, and shortly after we are being carried swiftly through the city. My foreign appearance attracts crowds, who gaze curiously after us until we are out of sight.

A Pack-horse Goes by Led by a Native with Straw Sandals and Hatless.

Our course is through the valley of Taubajegma, between ranges of beautiful mountains. We pass groups of children, who stare at me as though I were some wild animal.

Odd and interesting sights meet my eyes. The pack-horse goes by, led by a native with straw sandals, hatless and lightly clad. Curious and primitive is the merchandise thus carried, and the horse with his long forelock is no less striking. He, too, wears straw sandals, for the horses in Japan are never shod with iron shoes.

We cross the wooden bridge which spans the Saigawa. Only a few weeks since there was a great freshet here, sweeping away many of the houses, and injuring the crops. Now our way is through rice-fields; then in a twinkling we are surrounded by fields of the white mulberry, the food of the silk-worm. Our little wagons stand well this turning and twisting through field and lane, and the hard usage of the rough roads. Now and then we stop and pay toll; I wonder why, unless it is for the privilege of seeing the many curious sights which the route offers. At the end of our journey we are received by our host in the front porch of his house. After the customary ceremony of bowing, we are given leather cushions to sit upon.

One day I asked my guide the meaning of the repeated bows with which friends and relatives always greet each other. He replied that the first bow signifies that they wish each other well; the second that they have heard that the friend just met was in town; and the third that they are delighted to find this true, as they wished greatly to see him; the final bow is simply one of courtesy. This is the invariable ceremony with all classes, high and low, rich and poor.

Our hospitable host at once, as is the custom, places before us a pot of tea, and little cups. Then we talk of many things, the guide acting as interpreter. After a pleasant visit, we proceed to the house of another friend, a Mr. Ikebana, an artist in the arrangement of flowers in vases. The specimens of his skill in view evince a high order of taste, and I feel confident that many a drawing-room in Philadelphia would receive an acquisition to be proud of in one of these beautifully arranged vases.

We then visited Mr. Rankey Tanaka, noted as one of the most brilliant and successful artists in this province. Upon his walls are many panels painted by himself, which seem to me very high types of Japanese art. The ideas of artists and poets in Japan are quite different from those of talented men in Europe and America. While the latter are only too anxious to advertise and sell their productions, the Japanese masters will paint as few as possible—in fact, only as many as are necessary for a livelihood; for, they say, if they should flood the market with their works they would become common and unattractive.

One by one friends drop in, until eight gentlemen are seated upon cushions on the floor of a room facing a pretty Japanese garden. In the centre of our circle is a small table, about six inches high, filled with such delicacies as rice, saké, raw eggs, soup, fish, and pickles. This is considered a Japanese feast. Our party represents the general mercantile and literary element of the neighborhood, consisting of two artists, the village attorney, a capitalist, a gentleman deeply interested in silk culture and manufacture, and several farmers, beside the guide and myself. I notice at least thirty little heads peeping through the bushes that surround the garden, and ask the guide if there is a school in the vicinity. He answers in the negative, apparently surprised at my question. We have our tiffin, and chat for about two hours, in which time I have a good opportunity to observe their social manners. My guide is a great favorite, and entertains the party with his jokes and remarks on the odd manners and customs of the Americans. In response to their interest I tell them how Americans give a banquet, and how, instead of bowing and bowing, we extend the hand and shake it with a firm grip; and then I illustrate this by shaking hands with every one of them in true American fashion, squeezing their hands with much force. They yell out, and declare that I am a very powerful man, and after that I can see that some of them are rather timid about approaching me too closely. Before leaving I am laden with presents, according to the custom of the country. I receive beautiful samples of raw silk, delicately wrapped, with something written in Japanese on the outside; fresh eggs in a basket of plaited straw, a bottle of saké and a quantity of fruit. As I stand there with my arms full, truly, I feel like a beggar. As the finishing stroke, the artist steps forward, and hands me two beautifully-executed paintings, each about five feet long and two and one-half feet wide. He has painted upon the margin of one of them an original poem in honor of the occasion, and adorned it with a stamp bearing his crest, and his private and official signatures. Who can exceed in kindness and hospitality the people of this country?

Instead of saying "Sayonara" (good-bye), these gentlemen accompany us on our walk to the silk factory, Kawanakagimas, in the village of Otsuka, about a mile away. I appreciate their kindness.

On the way we pass the village graveyard; also, a shrine and a temple. We are received at the factory by the manager, who freely answers all my questions as to the growing and spinning of silk. We then walk through the spinning-room, a room fully one hundred feet long, in which sit about a hundred young Japanese girls, from thirteen to eighteen years of age, winding by machinery the silk from the cocoons upon spindles or spools.

After observing this process for some time, we all assemble in the front office, and form a circle, sitting upon the floor. In the centre is a huge pot of choice tea, from which we fill our cups. We sit here for half an hour, then prepare to take our departure. I shake hands with each in turn, saying "Good-bye," which they repeat, with broad smiles and great satisfaction.

As we walk about the village, I attract unusual atten-

Odd and Interesting Sights Meet My Eyes.

tion, and am followed by many of the natives. I ask the guide why I am such a curiosity, and he assures me that an American has never been seen in this village before.

We return to our jinrikishas, and are soon speeding homeward. The jinrikisha men have a curious way of notifying one another of the dangerous holes or rocks in the road. The leader calls out "E-o! E-o!" This is repeated in turn by those following until the last man utters the strange cry.

The night-watchman in Japan, more especially in the villages and small towns, follows an ancient custom of striking two sticks, called Hioshigi, or "tune-blocks," together as he makes his rounds. You can hear the clicking noise all through the night. The hour is also sounded thus: If it is three o'clock, the sticks are struck quickly three times; if half past three, then, after a second, they are struck once for the half-hour. The sticks are made of hard wood, and the name of the hotel or inn is carved upon them. This is an excellent custom, and one can be sure of the time-pieces, which is not always the case with those of the American watch-watch, or the electric clocks.

NOTE.—From the egg of the silk-worm the worm is hatched, and the cocoon made within forty days in the spring season. The same process in summer requires twenty days, while in the autumn it requires twenty-two or twenty-three days. Thus three crops a year may be secured.

The prices paid to the girls in the factory are as follows: Experienced hands, seven yen a month (equivalent to three and one-half dollars, United States currency). Inexperienced hands, one yen a month.

Food of rice is furnished in both cases. The time of labor is fourteen hours a day.

The average city wages of carpenters, working eight hours a day, are fifty sen. Laborers receive thirty sen and stone-cutters eighty sen in summer and seventy-five sen in winter.

In all cases men find themselves in food and clothing.

In the country men laborers are paid one yen, or fifty cents a month, and are furnished with food and clothing.

ON THE ROAD—AKAKURA—NAOETSU—NIIGATA.

Akakura—Hot springs—Eating with chopsticks—A warm bath—Blackened teeth—Naoetsu—Equalization of labor—Umbrellas—Katamachi—The new railroad—Aomigawa—Kashiwazaki—An inn receipt—Souvenirs—Jinrikisha rates—A "corner" in jinrikishas—Tashiro—Miyamoto—Yoita—Floods and freshets—Prayers for clear weather—A Japanese steamer.

WE leave Nagano this morning at 9.30 by train for Akakura, en route for Naoetsu. How beautiful, from the car window, is the view of the lofty mountains, with the wide plains at their feet! At Toyono we have a clear sight of Tojakushi-san and Ken-no-mine mountains, and last in the grand triad comes Myoko-zan, with its elevation of eight thousand one hundred and eighty feet. These mountains overlook a beautiful valley.

The grade is now upward until we reach Kashiwabara Station, at an altitude of two thousand two hundred feet. We do not stop again until we arrive at Akakura, when we leave the train, and after refreshing ourselves with a cup of tea at a neighboring inn we leave our baggage in the care of the landlady, and take jinrikishas for the celebrated Hot Springs, four miles distant.

On the way we pass a small settlement, which was only a few days ago a prosperous hamlet, but is now a mass of charred ruins. The entire population is at work, endeavoring to rebuild their wrecked homes.

In this section women and girls work equally with the men.

The road is up and down hills, which makes it hard for the jinrikisha men. Of course, when the hills are very steep, we relieve them by walking. At the springs we have clean and comfortable quarters on the second floor of the best inn, Kogaku-ro. Tiffin is served in Japanese fashion, with chopsticks. How awkward they are, in eating rice and soup! However, I make a good lunch of hot rice, fish, soup, and some small sweetmeats.

After tiffin, we take a short nap, then prepare for a hot bath in water that flows directly from the heart of the mountain. We are shown to a small room on the ground floor, about twenty-five feet square, in the centre of which is a tub, about ten feet square and four feet deep. Here we make our first dip into mineral water at a temperature of at least one hundred and twenty-

---

NOTE.—At all inns, chopsticks are furnished with the meal. You will find upon the tray holding the meal, a nice new pair enclosed in a paper napkin. They are cut in such a manner that the tops are still joined together, and when broken apart, a toothpick is found secreted between them.

five degrees. When we emerge, some ten minutes later, we look like boiled lobsters. Two little girls bring us towels, and we return to our room to rest after this boiling process.

In my room again, I call for some hot tea, and the little Neisan sits beside me, fanning me while I drink, as is the custom here. I observe that the teeth of this girl are blackened, and conclude that she is married. Upon my guide asking her if this is the case, she replies that she is not married, but that she blackens her teeth because she is twenty-four, and too old to marry. It is the custom here for married women, and maidens, when too old to marry, to blacken the teeth. The stain used for this purpose is made of iron juice and powdered fruit. The process is called Chaguro, or iron gate.

The Japanese think that when a woman speaks, she spoils everything, and so the blackened teeth are supposed to give them the appearance of closed lips. Young girls powder the face, paint the cheeks and lips, and whiten the teeth.

A short distance from the inn is the public bath-house. Within this building men and women bathe together. In some bath-houses a bamboo pole is stretched across the bath to separate the men and women, but this is not regarded, for men and women sit and talk together on the side of the tub in the most unconventional manner.

It is customary for the proprietor of the inn at which you stop for tea or rice, especially if he and his servants have been liberally supplied with chai-dai, or "tea-money," to walk a short distance down the road, and stand there till you pass, bowing profoundly, and saying "Arigato!" (thank you), and "Sayonara" (good-bye). At 4.50 P. M. we take the train at Akakura station for Naoetsu, and arrive there in two hours. This is the terminus of the railroad.

At the Iga Inn here I am honored with the best, or "gold" room, commanding a very pretty garden, which is reserved for distinguished guests. And, as usual, the landlady appears with profound bows, her head touching the ground, with profuse apologies for her inconvenient rooms, and the poor service of her house.

When traveling in the interior of Japan, one must learn to do without milk, butter, meats of all kinds, bread and water, and confine his diet to rice, tea, fish, eggs, and saké.

Water in Japan is unwholesome from the fact that the rice fields, which are generally irrigated, are heavily covered with human manure, and the streams cannot escape infection. An excellent drink is made of barley, baked and steeped in hot water, as tea, without sugar.

We spend a couple of days at Naoetsu, arranging for our trip by jinrikisha and on foot to Niigata. It is necessary for each jinrikisha to have two extra men, as the roads are rough, and hard to pull over, especially as far as the first village, where we change our men. We hope to reach Yoita, a distance of fifty-five miles, before night, if it does not rain.

Since leaving Naoetsu, the sky has clouded over, and we are threatened with rain. We pass through many small villages, where we notice that only a few of the houses have thatched roofs, the others being mostly of shingles, upon which are placed heavy cobble-stones, to prevent them from being blown away by the violent winds that frequent these districts during the winter season.

Our road is the main thoroughfare, and eyes and fingers are kept busy taking notes. Women and girls are as great workers as the men in this province. They are strong and muscular. I was amused to see a little, brown-skinned girl, about seven or eight years old, trying to carry a log fully as large as herself to a neighboring wood-pile. The early training of these children gives them strength and endurance. The large forms of the women would naturally impress one with the idea that they were incapable of hard labor, but this is not the case; they can stand all kinds of work and weather. Like the men, they invariably carry their tobacco pouches and pipes at their sides, for smoking is a national custom, common to men, women, and children.

The road is being repaired, and for miles we run over a kind of slag, which renders travel rough, unpleasant, and tedious. Thus far we have passed only shanties, there being no good houses in this section of the country. In many villages there are rows of these shanties bordering the streets, with the closets directly in front of them. The drainage of these places is bad, and one can easily account for the dreadful odors which greet us as we pass through. Not only are diseases and dirt prevalent, but at many of the shops quantities of unripe fruit are exposed for sale, and costing but a trifle, are indulged in by the young people to the extent of their pocket-books.

The large straw hat is generally worn here, although many of the women have only a towel over their heads. Heavy wooden shoes and straw sandals are common, and just as universal are the oiled paper umbrellas carried by pilgrims and other pedestrians to protect them from the sun and rain. Many of the inns loan these umbrellas to their patrons. Such have the name of the inn painted conspicuously on the cover in the sign language of Japan. Individuals also have their names upon their umbrellas, so that it would not be an easy thing to steal one of them and escape detection. Should one require an extra hamper, a very excellent one can be purchased at any of the villages. These are called " Kori," and are made of straw and sold at a low price.

By the roadside are many simple Shinto shrines, made by placing one large stone upright upon another, and a cheaply constructed torii in front. It is not uncommon to see the natives kneeling before these shrines, praying to the deity whom the sacred images represent.

Our first stop, since leaving Naoetsu, is at the village of Katamachi, which is not unlike the other villages through which we have passed. It is astonishing how the jinrikisha men will jog along with their burden, never stopping to rest or take breath until the journey is completed. At this village we take a short rest and a cup of tea at a tea house, then move forward with fresh jinrikisha men and wagons. We pass thus from village to village, changing our men and wagons at the end of every five or ten miles.

As usual, I attract much attention in all these places. At Katamachi I am surrounded by a number of villagers, among them a young girl, who is so much excited by my strange appearance that she runs across the street to her home, and brings back with her two old women and a couple of sisters, all of whom stand staring and laughing at me until I am out of sight.

We skirt the ocean front for miles and miles, then follow a path about a quarter of a mile inland. We can now see the island of Sado on our left, about fifteen miles from the mainland.

The number of children in this part of the country

is enormous. The older ones are poorly clad, and many of the younger ones are quite naked. This seems to be the most prolific of all the crops raised on these islands.

The Hokuitsu Railroad Company is building, with private capital, a line from Naoetsu to Niigata, a distance of eighty-four miles. The proposed route skirts the ocean, close to the main road. All along our way, men, women, and girls are at work upon it, the women, equally with the men, carrying bricks, earth, or stones in baskets suspended from long poles across their shoulders. It is a strange sight, and somewhat sad, to see a strong, pretty, and attractive girl carrying great loads of brick and stone. We also see hundreds of women and girls picking and shoveling dirt. I have thought that the life of the factory girl in America is bad enough, but it is pleasant, compared with that of these poor souls.

Stopping the jinrikisha, I ask what are the wages of these poor people, and am informed that the railroad company pays them twenty sen, or ten cents a day, providing also rice and other cheap articles of food. The hours of work are from sunrise to sunset. What a life of slavery, with no prospect of anything easier as they grow older!

After we leave the village of Kakizaki, the route is more mountainous. In many places the grade is so steep that we are obliged to walk, while the men pull the wagons after us. The best way to travel through the interior is to send jinrikisha men ahead with the luggage, to engage men and carriages for the following stage, thus saving time and trouble.

The wide expanse of ocean, together with the rugged rocks, forms a beautiful picture. Now we climb the side of a mountain, looking down upon the village through which we have just passed. Here and there we can see where the tunnels of the new railroad will penetrate the mountains, and all along the route is constantly heard the sound of blasting rocks, and the hum of busy laborers upon the various sections of the road. Over each batch of natives is placed an overseer, who takes good care that there is no lagging in the work. The laborers are lightly clad, but are prohibited by law from appearing in a nude state. When the days are hot, as to-day, this law is not strictly observed, and it is not uncommon to see, within the inns, women, naked from the waist up, and men without a vestige of clothing.

The heat is oppressive. I find the temperature to be 90° under my umbrella and 106° in the sun, and yet I do not suffer as one would suppose in this temperature. I think the foreigner stands it quite as well as and even better than the natives, whom I see lying around by dozens and apparently prostrated by the heat. At Hachisaki we take tea as usual and change men and wagons. There is always much laughter among the jinrikisha men at these changes, as they survey dubiously my "great size and weight." I am looked upon by these Japanese as a gigantic and powerful personage. The natives, both men and women, are small and of light weight.

Beyond the village the road is more mountainous, and we do much walking up the steep heights. This part of the journey is full of enjoyment. The activity of the laborers upon the new road, their odd manner of working, and their strange tools, the many pilgrims wandering to and from some noted shrine or temple, all are interesting sights. At times we meet numbers of people returning from a religious festival, scrambling over the mountains to their village homes.

We rest and change men at Aomigawa, having made twenty-four and a half miles since leaving Naoetsu this morning. The tea house at which we stop is beautifully situated on the side of the mountain, one thousand feet above the sea. From this point we have a fine bird's-eye view of the ocean and the surrounding country. The air is fresh and bracing.

It is now 12.30 P. M., and we have been moving constantly for five hours and a half. My guide prepares a good lunch of rice, eggs, canned meat, and a pot of tea. He carries it to a bench overlooking the sea, where we rest for three-quarters of an hour, then continue our way between long ranges of mountains on one side and the Japan Sea on the other, which, with many strange customs and costumes of the people we meet, gives continual variety to the journey. Since leaving Naoetsu we have not seen a foreigner; in fact, but two since leaving Nikko.

Rain now comes on, and we have made only the short half of our day's journey. It is so violent, and as there is no prospect of clearing weather we decide to remain over night at the nearest village. It is not pleasant to be thoroughly drenched while traveling in this part of the country, where the sun is the only means of drying one's clothing.

It is half-past two in the afternoon, and we enter the village of Kashiwazaki, thirty miles from Naoetsu. We go directly to the Iwatoya, or Rock Gate house, the best inn in the place, where we pass a very comfortable night. Rising at five o'clock, we partake of a breakfast of boiled rice and raw eggs, and at 6.30 are again on the road. It is still wet and unpleasant, with no signs of clearing. Oiled wraps and waterproofs are at hand, and rain is never allowed to delay the traveler in Japan, or interfere with the carrying out of his plans. There are a few things that might stir up his nerves, such as earthquakes, floods, and tidal waves. The first two of these I have experienced to some extent; the latter, fortunately, never.

An "inn receipt," as they call it, more properly a letter of introduction, is given by the hosts or land-ladies of inns to their patrons on leaving, when requested. We find these letters of great advantage in going from inn to inn, and in engaging men and wagons.

Every inn in Japan has, according to law, a printed or written notice hanging upon its wall, stating its rates for meals and lodgings. These rates are first, second, third, and fourth class.

It is also customary for the landlord or landlady to present to the guest a souvenir at parting, such as elaborately printed towels, boxes made of lacquered wood, small picture-books, and the like. I have quite a collection of these little gifts.

The legal rate for jinrikisha men throughout the country is seven sen per ri, a distance of two and forty-four one-hundredths English statute miles, or, roughly speaking, a trifle under two and one-half miles. The native of Japan pays at this rate, whether he is heavy or light in weight, but foreigners are always charged more, because, it is said, they are much heavier than the natives, and are generally in a great hurry, compelling the men to go on a trot instead of a walk. Therefore a rate of nine and one-half sen per ri is demanded. These jinrikisha men will run, on a stretch, at an average of seven and eight miles an hour, pulling a passenger of medium weight. Should the passenger be heavy, two men are necessary. Our men have frequently run seven and one-half miles an hour, two men to each wagon, up and down a hilly road. I have also had two men pull me twelve miles without making a single stop, the entire distance being covered at a trotting gait.

It is sometimes amusing, and somewhat annoying, upon our arrival at a village where a change is to be made, to find the men trying to put us in a "hole," as it were. At one of the places, the four men that we required were all disabled (?). One had a very bad headache, a wet towel being tied around his head. One had stomach-ache, and could hardly walk; the third was so sick, sitting down with his head between his hands; the fourth had sore feet. After an hour's delay I asked the guide what we were to do? He laughed, and said they had a "corner" in jinrikishas in that village, and that a letter of introduction to the inn would not avail to heal these poor men's ailments. However, the offer of an extra sen per mile soon cured the afflicted creatures, and with that salve applied to their various diseases, we were soon flying along at a more rapid pace than heretofore. Money is a good medicine, which must be freely administered if one desires to make haste in slow Japan. The demands, however, are moderate, and the railroads now in process of construction throughout the country, will render the traveler more independent in the future.

The jinrikisha men are generally small and slender, but quite muscular. They live almost entirely upon

Here are Two Girls at a Well, Drawing Water.

rice, fish, raw eggs, and tea. One's first experience of jinrikisha riding naturally gives him a feeling of great sympathy for these men in their laborious work, but when he becomes accustomed to this mode of traveling, with all its vicissitudes and impositions, pity is frequently left in the background, and the little human horses are treated simply as beasts of burden.

We reach the village of Sochi in an hour, making a distance of nearly seven and one-half miles. We are passing through a flat and uninteresting part of the country; but the interesting people that we meet, and the odd-looking houses and their surroundings, in the many villages through which we pass, vary the monotony of the journey. In a number of places the entire life of the people within the houses is exposed to public view, and thus we are witnesses of curious sights. Here, near a little cottage of one story, are two girls at a well, drawing water and washing their tubs and buckets, and looking very quaint and picturesque in their native costumes.

Here a coolie is carrying great bundles upon a sort of wooden chair strapped to his back, and looking, as usual, heavy and unintelligent.

We halt and change at the village of Tashiro. As we ride along we see women and girls pushing great loads in heavy carts. Sometimes a small boy is in front, holding up the shafts. I have seen loads, considered heavy for strong horses, pushed thus by a woman and a boy, up and down hills, for miles over the country.

At Miyamoto we find a nice clean tea house, and are served by two pretty Neisan, who laugh merrily, and seem to think I am a very strange sort of being. In all these villages the tea houses are so much alike, in-

A COOLIE CARRYING GREAT BUNDLES UPON A SORT OF WOODEN CHAIR.

side and out, that one can almost believe that he returns again and again to the same place.

In winter snow often falls in this region to a depth

of from three to five feet, and remains long on the ground, owing to the extremely cold weather. In these cases the streets are scarcely used at all, the people passing from place to place under the small sheds in front of their houses.

Here are large fields of the Kara, which is used in making thatched roofs. It is mixed in equal quantities with rice straw, and is said to form a roof of enduring quality, cool in summer and warm in winter.

We have reached our last station, Yoita, in the village of Hara, where we take a small steamer for Niigata, about forty miles distant, hoping to arrive at six o'clock this evening. As the steamer does not leave her dock until one o'clock, we have plenty of time for rest and refreshment. Our run from Kashiwazaki this morning was about twenty-four miles.

There have been great floods and freshets in this district. The neighboring rivers have risen to such an extent, owing to the heavy rains of July, that for miles and miles fields, roads, and houses are wholly or in part covered with water, making the country look desolate and doing much injury to the crops. Carpenters and other workmen are seen at all points, repairing the damages to field and property. Being near some of these men, I request my guide to ask them what wages they are paid, and am informed that they receive fifteen sen, or seven and one-half cents a day, if food is supplied; without food they are paid thirty sen a day.

This is quite an anxious time in Japan on account of the advanced state of the rice crop, and the probability of it being ruined by continued rain. Prayers for clear weather are offered at all the shrines and temples by the country people. At many of the larger villages religious festivals are held, and the various gods are besought to withhold their wrath. I have seen several of the processions going to or returning from their places of worship. From present indications their appeals do not seem to be having the desired effect, for we are having much rain, and the crops are in danger of being wholly destroyed.

It is time for our steamer. Hearing a shrill whistle, I look down the river, and see a very small vessel coming towards the landing. In a few moments she is abreast of us, and a large board is laid from the bank to her deck. The river is the Shinano-gawa, which empties into the Sea of Japan at Niigata. It is very wide and shallow, and experience and judgment are necessary to navigate its waters, even with this small craft. It is interesting to watch the country people go aboard, in their scanty clothing, with their queer-looking bundles and hand-satchels. They follow each other in single file across the plank and into the cabins, which are first and second class.

A Japanese steamer is different from those in our country. Of the two cabins, the fore cabin is for first-class passengers, the aft cabin for those of the second class. These cabins are devoid of all furniture. Matting covers the floor, and in the first-class cabins there are leather cushions. Those of the second class have no cushions. In the centre of each is a hibashi, or charcoal fire, from which the passengers receive some heat, and by which they light their pipes. The men and women huddle together. The captain, whose quarters are above the lower cabins, invites me to go up there with my guide. He offers me a sort of a bench upon which I sit, and have a fine view from his windows of the country in which I am so much interested.

MOUNTAIN ROADS—JINRIKISHA MEN—AND RAIN.

On a Japanese steamer — Aground — Niigata — Change of route — Photographing the tea girls — Kameda — Universal Panacea — Bad roads — Jinrikisha men on a strike — Tobacco fields — Yasuda — Tiffin — A curious crowd — Komatsu — Deep Gully — the Aganogawa — Dangerous road — Kuroiwa Pass — Mountain echo — An overturned jinrikisha — Tsugawa — Pipes at night — Japanese toothbrushes — Spectacles — Too much rain — Wax tree — Cedars and cryptomerias — Torii Pass — Worse and worse — Nozawa — Wakamatsu — Tabanematsu tunnel — Bridge of boats — Crossing the bridge — Bange.

WITH a shrill whistle we are off; the boat is propelled by two wooden paddles. From my window I see in the distance hundreds of men and women repairing a dyke with strange-looking machines. There are several tall derricks and huge stone hammers, the latter being lifted by strong ropes. Some fifty of the workmen run along, pulling the end of the rope, and uttering loud shouts. When the hammer is lifted to the top of the derrick, they let go the rope, with another shout, and the heavy weight falls upon the pile below. This operation is repeated again and again until the pile is firmly driven.

Shortly after this we run aground. I wonder what now? The little steamer puffs and sends forth great volumes of steam, and makes a great fuss generally, but does not move an inch. Now the captain, with four or five men and long bamboo poles, push and push, but the boat seems only the more deeply imbedded in the mud. One of the crew strips off his cotton shirt and jumps overboard to take soundings, of which the captain makes a note. Steam is again put on, and the boat turns, as if on a pivot. At last she is released, and to our joy we are once more steaming down the river. Where the stream is so shallow that it will not admit of the passage of a steamboat we change to a sampan, rowboats being provided for baggage and other freight.

I excite as much interest in the passengers as they do in me, and we look at each other in mutual wonder. At Sangeo village we are transferred to another steamer, and again, after going a short distance, we change to a new and larger vessel. This captain is as friendly as his predecessors, and I share his room in the wheelhouse above the cabins. Every passenger seems to have the privilege of talking to him and his assistants, especially when they are most seriously engaged in steering the steamer through the channel, and past projecting rocks. But he is very polite, and answers all questions with a smile. I am filled with admiration for his good nature.

Here are neither lights nor buoys to direct the navigator. The river is wide at this point, the shallow places being made navigable by a series of dykes along the banks.

It is 7.30 P. M., and we can see the lights of Niigata in the distance. One-half hour more, and we are safely landed with our baggage. As we enter the streets, the shouting from the throats of at least fifty jinrikisha men reminds me of Liberty Street ferry, in the city of New York.

Niigata is an open port, with a population of over thirty-three thousand souls. It was opened to foreign trade in 1869.

Calling for two jinrikishas, a half-a-dozen answer us, and a great jabbering as to who will take us follows. The discussion is finally settled by one of the men taking from his pocket six pieces of cord, one of which he hands to each of the contestants. Each man holds one end of his cord; the other ends are twisted together. Then the arbitrator steps forward, and takes hold of two of the loose ends. The men holding the corresponding ends take us in their jinrikishas, and we are quickly carried to the best inn, the Yoshi-kwan.

Sunday, September 6th.—The day is rainy, and the thermometer seventy-two in the shade. I devote the day to rest and letter-writing, also to the discussion of plans of travel with my guide. Sundays are not especially sacred in Japan. All days with them are alike, **and they work the whole seven days of the week.**

After tiffin, we stretch ourselves upon the floor, and, with maps before us, plan out the best route. The recent heavy storms and freshets have washed many of the mountain roads, so that they are at present impassable.

This information compels us to change materially the route of our mountain trip to Sendai. We therefore decide to leave here to-morrow by a small steamer for Kameda, thence by 'rikisha to Tsugawa, Wakamatsu and Motomiya. At the latter point we strike the railroad, by which we go to Fuku-Shima, Shiogama, Matsushima, Morioka and Aomori. Our line of travel may extend over a larger portion of the country, and in other directions. This will depend upon the condition of the rivers and roads.

Before leaving Niigata, I ask the landlord's permission to photograph some of his tea-girls. He calls up those who have waited upon me during my stay here, and directs them to stand in the garden, near my room. I make several photographs of them.

At the landing a little steam launch is waiting to convey us to Kameda, a distance of seven and one-half miles. My guide and I sit upon the roof of the cabin, and my feet, dangling over in their American shoes, seem to afford much amusement to the young Japanese ladies within the cabin. We take this boat through the Horinoki-gawa canal, then go by jinrikisha over a road running parallel with the canal. First-class fare for one person is ten sen.

Strange sights meet our eyes. The hour being early, 8.30 A. M., there are numbers of women washing clothes in the canal, while boys and girls are bathing their little brown bodies, enjoying meanwhile much sport. Dozens of sampans, of various shapes, are pushed along the water by men and women with long bamboo poles. Their cargoes are stone ballast, vegetables, and merchandise.

We arrive at Kameda in an hour, and go at once to the best inn in the village. At these first-class inns you have the advantage of securing honest and reliable jinrikisha men, the cha-dai, or tea-money, being considered by the proprietor sufficient payment for his influence in your behalf.

As usual, good men are here recommended, and we flatter ourselves that we are ready to start, when, rain having set in, the men absolutely refuse to go, saying the roads are muddy, and hard to pull over. The jinrikisha men in this section are well-to-do, and more independent than those at Yokohama, Tokyo, and other large cities. I see that they again have a "corner" which only the Universal Panacea can open. An extra sen per ri soon overcomes their disinclination, and we are off at a good pace.

A comely young girl sat in the inn while my guide

was bargaining with the landlady, and, rather to my surprise, I was subsequently informed that she was flirting with me. These girls have a peculiar way of flirting, which can be appreciated only by a personal experience in this country.

In many of the houses of Kameda we see young girls spinning. Only young girls are employed in this work. The district is noted for the abundance of cotton and tobacco raised. The rain now comes down in earnest, but we are well protected by wrap and covering, which is a source of great satisfaction, for many of the jinrikishas are in bad condition, and the occupants experience considerable discomfort when it rains.

We stop at a small tea house in the village of Ounkiu, where we again have trouble in securing men to carry us forward. We have anticipated this, however, for before leaving Niigata we learned of the dreadful condition of the roads, and the refusal of the men to draw passengers. But the universal remedy once more proves successful, and we continue our journey.

The country here is flat and uninteresting. We pass many pilgrims and other pedestrians on the thoroughfare. The dress of the men and women is uniform, consisting of tight-fitting trousers and a loose coat, with a large straw hat or a towel tied on the head.

We pass large fields of tobacco, and see upon the sides of the houses quantities of the tobacco-leaf hung up to dry. Now and then we meet a cart laden with tobacco, and drawn by a bull. Instead of a yoke, such as we use in America, a wooden stick or board rests upon the neck of the animal.

By this time the rain is coming down in torrents. After a hard pull through very soft and uneven roads,

NOW AND THEN WE MEET A CART LADEN WITH TOBACCO AND DRAWN BY A BULL.

we reach a tea house in the village Yasuda in time for tiffin.

While I am eating my rice and eggs, a dozen boys and girls are peeping through the window at me, and not satisfied that they alone should see this curious stranger eating with a knife and fork, they run off, and soon return accompanied by a score of older people, who stare and wonder with wide eyes, standing like statues. I request the guide to disperse this crowd, which he promptly does, and I finish the meal in comfort.

At Komatsu we have still greater difficulty in procuring men. The landlord of our inn uses all his influence, but it is of no avail. The men flatly refuse to take us. There seems to be a contention among them. I hear earnest and loud talking, and the guide tells me they are having a "hot time." They tell us that the road beyond us is impassable, in consequence of washouts and fallen bridges, and that if they start they will be compelled to turn back. Still we are not discouraged, and my guide asks me what we shall do?

I say we will push on, even if we must walk. After a long time, and just as we are about to carry out this resolution, the men come to us, and say that they will take us if we will pay twenty sen per ri to each man. This is double any price that we have yet paid, and nearly three times the fare allowed by law. However, we engage them, and set out. Henceforward we have a good deal of sharp bargaining at every village where a change is made.

It is really pitiable to see these men pulling their heavy loads over the rough and muddy roads, which grow worse with every mile. We bounce from side to side, and apparently are only by chance saved from upsetting. Should this state of affairs continue, we will be compelled either to walk, or give up this route altogether. Even now many places are so badly washed that we often walk a mile at a time, when we are completely drenched.

We reach Nakasendo after much difficulty and delay. The view here is picturesque and beautiful. Tall mountains surround us, and the lovely Agano-gawa flows at their feet. No one would think that this peaceful stream, only a few weeks ago, caused such fearful havoc and destruction to homes and property.

The road is becoming impassable, and my guide tells me that there is much grumbling among the men for having come, even at the excessive rate of twenty sen per ri. We now walk still more frequently, where the road is badly washed. Here we must cross a long, stout plank, which has been placed over a deep hollow. The men follow with the wagons on their backs. At many places the path is very narrow, and I think if there should be a landslide, or even should we make a misstep, we would be precipitated a hundred feet into the river below.

The little village of Igaskima is a charming spot. Mountains of the same name rise far above us. The rain is pouring down upon us, and our next stopping-place is still five miles distant. We are anxious lest the night should come upon us before we reach it. Without lamps, and the road in such a condition, we would indeed be in a dangerous plight.

Suddenly a deep gully appears, fully forty feet wide, with a narrow foot-bridge over it. We step upon it cautiously, and the men follow with the wagons, using the utmost care, for a slip here would mean the total destruction of their frail burdens, and possibly loss of life. However, we all pass over in safety. The scenery grows more and more beautiful, combining river and mountain in grand and rugged effect.

Now we have trouble indeed, for the large bridge, a hundred feet long and fifteen feet wide, has been swept from its foundations, and carried by the freshet to a distance of twenty feet, where it is twisted to an angle of forty-five degrees, with the wild and rapid current under it. This is a sad predicament. What shall we do? We must push onward, for the distance is too great to turn back. After a consultation, we decide that our six jinrikisha men must carry their wagons over as best they can, and we will try to creep over. Dangerous and almost impossible as this looks, we finally accomplish it, and after an hour of hard work find ourselves safe and sound on the other side.

Kuroiwa Pass is a scene worthy of an artist's brush. Above us on our right is the rocky Kobanji, and at its base a tunnel one hundred and fifty feet long, which we now enter. As we go through, our men utter loud shouts, and the echo responds to the different voices.

The mountains here are extremely precipitous, and dangerous for pedestrians. We follow the course of the Agano-gawa, as it winds its way over a rocky bed, accompanied by the lofty mountains. The way is so dark and rough that, fearing an accident, I get out and walk. The guide follows my example, and it is well that he does, for not ten minutes later one of the jinrikishas turns over, and all its contents are thrown in the mud. A pretty sight!

And what has become of my cameras and plates? I fear much damage will be the result of this wet and hazardous expedition. I am thankful that it was not one of us that received such ill treatment. At Kiyokawa we leave the jinrikishas behind, but take the men to carry our baggage. We are taken over to the town of Tsugawa in a small row-boat, and reach a good inn here at eight o'clock. We have traveled seven miles and a half by steamer, and thirty-two and three-quarters miles by jinrikisha, through rain and over bad roads, to-day.

As our men are tired, and it is late for them to return to their village, I arrange for their supper and lodging, with breakfast at the inn, for which they show their appreciation by profound bows. The accommodations here are not of the best, as we find in these regions only inns of purely Japanese character. As I lie in my bed on the floor, thinking of the many advantages and comforts of home, I am annoyed by the continual tap, tap, tap of pipes, and by weird, unpleasant music and songs, until late in the night. The clicking noise at intervals of one or two minutes is caused by the smokers striking their pipes upon a bamboo box in the hibashi to empty them.

Another strange sight, and one constantly met with, is the enormous smoked-glass spectacles worn by the natives of Japan, to protect their eyes from the sun. These spectacles are fully two inches in diameter, and perfectly round, giving the wearer a very peculiar appearance. However, in time one becomes accustomed to all these odd sights, and ceases to wonder at anything.

We pass an uncomfortable night, for our clothing is quite wet from the day's exposure. After a breakfast of hot rice, eggs, and tea, we leave Tsugawa at half-past seven o'clock, hoping to reach Wakamatsu before nightfall. I am disappointed to find it raining hard, and as we will pass on the way some of the most beautiful mountain scenery, this fact will interfere considerably with my photographing.

NOTE.—One sees queer tooth-brushes when traveling in the interior. They are made of sticks of wood, the size of a lead pencil, sharpened at one end for a tooth-pick, while on the other end is a sort of a mop. The brushes are thrown away after being used once. They are sold in packages of a dozen, at two or three sen a bunch.

I thank my stars, while traveling in Japan, and especially during this rainy season, that there is such a medicine as quinine, to which I attribute the prevention of colds and other troubles, consequent upon exposure to this unfamiliar climate. The country about us is wild and picturesque, reminding me of the mountain scenery in central Pennsylvania. Here are numbers of small trees, called wax trees, from which the famous lacquer liquid, used so extensively by the Japanese in oil-finished woodwork, is made. Candles are also made from the seed. The roads in Japan are ballasted with small pebbles gathered from the rivers in the vicinity. In the absence of rivers, stone is brought from the mountains, and broken into small pieces, such as we do on our country roads.

Here are forests of cedars and cryptomerias. We pass acre after acre of this valuable wood. Cedar is extensively used in building houses, and especially for the floors of inns. It is never painted or varnished, but planed and finished to a high degree of perfection, and being constantly traveled over by "stocking feet," acquires a fine polish.

It is a curious fact that the women of Japan, of all ranks, walk with their feet turned in, and are generally bow-legged. I attribute this to the universal custom of sitting on their feet.

Again we see in the distance mountains, from fifteen

hundred to two thousand feet high, with their peaks enveloped in mist and clouds. I wonder if it will ever stop raining!

The way begins to ascend, and I learn that we are at the foot of Torii Pass. The road is barely passable, and deep gullies and ruts covered with mud and water render the tracks uncertain. We do not know how far we will sink in this mud, or whether we will not at any minute be hurled from the wagons. Our wheels sink deeper and deeper, and are extricated with difficulty. The rain comes in torrents, and the wind increases every moment. The men make frequent halts, for the pull is a hard one. Grand scenery is all about us, and as we climb higher and higher, we behold the summits of the neighboring mountains. The wind, by this time has become a gale, and I feel as though our wagons will surely be blown away. The tops of the jinrikishas and the oil-cloth coverings have entirely disappeared.

Upon reaching the mountain top, we find that we have been two hours in making the ascent. We rest at a tea house on the roadside, and give the men a lunch of rice, raw eggs, tea, and dried fish, the cost of which for six men is thirty sen, or fifteen cents of our money.

When we cross the boundary line, and pass into the province of Iwashiro, the road is horrible. Ruts twelve inches deep are seen on either side, and the mire is so thick and sticky that sometimes the efforts of the whole six men are necessary to release one wagon. As we descend, we pitch from side to side. How my man in the shafts bounds to and fro! I can scarcely keep my seat. But I take a firm grip, and do my best to hold on, feeling as though I am floating in a tub on an angry sea. This unpleasant motion ceases, to my great joy, and we enter a tea house in the village of Muraoka, at the foot of the Kuruma Pass. Since leaving Tsugawa, we have covered a distance of six ri, or about sixteen miles. We have yet eleven ri before us, ere we reach Wakamatsu.

At Muraoka we engage additional men, one for each wagon, making nine in all, and begin the ascent of another mountain pass, with the worst possible roads. My guide tells me that in his thirteen years' experience on the roads of Japan he has never seen any as bad as these. Even with the additional men, it is impossible to pull up the mountain passes, and we are two miles from the nearest tea house. The rain is coming down in sheets—" shot " rain they call it in Japan—and the only thing to be done is to get out and walk; so pulling a woollen blanket over my shoulders, and taking off my shoes, we set out, and make a tedious and laborious journey to the village of Nozawa, where we rest and eat a cold lunch.

We now place four men on each wagon, paying their demand of twenty sen per ri to each man. We are at the mercy of these men, and no one is better aware of the fact than they. Even with this number of men we are at times obliged to get out and walk. By this time I am seasick, or "jinrikisha" sick, for the constant and severe jolting has not only made me sick, but given me severe pains, which, however, I keep to myself. I am astonished at the rough usage our little wagons are capable of withstanding.

The rain does not abate in the least, and the mud and water in our way are appalling! Rivers and streams are rising, and great waterfalls rush madly by us, which in ordinary times are but small mountain streams or rivulets.

We have grave doubts as to whether we will reach Wakamatsu to-night. Our men show signs of fatigue, and we have no hope of relieving them, or adding to our force. The difficulties and delays have been innumerable. Our frequent halts, getting in and out of the wagons, and the poor coverings, have made us wet and chilly. I occasionally take a swallow of the Japanese rice whiskey, called saké, which, with quinine is a safeguard against cold. We have still twenty-three miles before us. The men are cheerful, and laugh or grunt, as they struggle on the way. The road increases in beauty, and it grieves me to think that I have a camera, yes, two of them, and a paint-box, and am unable to use any of them.

The oldest inhabitants inform me that they have never known such continued and severe rains as the present ones. We are now on a new road, which was built about a year ago by private capital, subscribed in the neighboring villages. The old road was so cut up by constant and heavy travel as to render it almost impassable for jinrikishas. As we descend the Tabanematsu Pass and mountain, a gradually widening panorama of wondrous beauty spreads itself out before us. Even in this great downpour of rain we halt several times for a parting glance at some exquisite bit of scenery. We are a thousand feet above the valley. The path is at times very narrow, and the water rushing over it and tumbling down the mountain side gives me a chill, as I think of my fate, should I follow this beckoning, all-sweeping flood, this whimsical mountain sprite, who seems to bewitch one's senses to-day, as in the olden times of fairy lore.

At the top of the mountain is a little tea house on the side of the road. Here we rest. A short distance from us is a tunnel in the mountain, only large enough for a jinrikisha to pass through. It is called the Tabanematsu Tunnel, and is seven hundred and eighty feet long. Our men carry lighted lamps, as we pass through it, for it is quite dark in the centre. Coming out on the other side, we have a fine bird's-eye view of the valley, which is completely surrounded by mountains.

We have given up all hope of reaching Wakamatsu to-night. In fact, at the last tea house at which we stopped we were informed that the Tadamikawa River is impassable, the bridge having been washed away. If this is the case, we are again cut short in our proposed route, and must turn back toward Nikko, for it is necessary to cross this river to continue our journey to Motomiya. With anxious thoughts I sit in my jinrikisha, hoping the reports are unfounded. It is now dark, and the men halt to light their lanterns of oiled paper.

We can hear the rush of the river long before its banks are in sight. At the village of Katakado, we learn that the risk of attempting to cross the river is great, as the temporary bridge is formed of a series of sampans, placed at distances of twenty feet apart, and held together by a huge steel cable, which extends from shore to shore. Upon these frail boats boards are loosely thrown, and these constitute the bridge.

We stand upon the shore and observe this turbulent mass of water. It is about two thousand feet across, and at this point has become a rapids. The risk is obvious, and we learn that only two parties have attempted crossing. Should the cable which holds these jumping boats together break, our fate would be a serious one.

I consider all things, and finally tell the guide we

will risk it. We engage several coolies, two of whom, bearing torches, are at the front and rear of our party, and wave their lights to and fro, making quite an illumination. After the first torchman, the other coolies follow with our baggage, then the guide, and lastly myself. Before starting, I take off my shoes, stockings, coat and vest, thinking, in case of accident, I will have more freedom of action without them. The planks are wet and slippery, and great care is required to balance ourselves upon the narrow footway, which is barely eighteen inches wide.

The darkness of the night around us adds to the danger of the undertaking, but we keep our heads cool, and proceed very slowly. How the little boats rise and toss about! Sometimes we all stand still, fearing, if we make a movement, to be pitched overboard. A false step would mean certain death. When half-way across, I glance at the water madly surging by, only five feet below us, and for an instant a panic overpowers me. What if the rope which holds these boats should give way? How foolish it was to attempt the crossing! However, after fifteen minutes of suspense and intense excitement we land, bag and baggage, on the opposite bank, unharmed by our daring venture.

In the village of Takatera we go to a tea house on the river bank, and there learn that to-day the river has risen six feet in five hours and a half.

I would not repeat the experiment we have just made. It is an extremely dangerous expedient, and as the river is still rising, I predict that the cable will not hold through the night.

After a tedious ride, we reach Bange at 9.15 P. M., wet, chilly, and exhausted, having traveled almost constantly for nearly fourteen hours, and covered a distance of fourteen ri, or about thirty-five miles.

We are now three ri, or seven and one-half miles, from Wakamatsu. In our wet clothing, with a scanty meal of rice, raw eggs, and tea, we try to make ourselves comfortable. There are no chairs, tables, or beds here. Every one must pay homage to the floor.

How I long for an easy chair, and a table upon which to write and eat my meals! How often I think of the comforts of home, the well-served meals, the savory meats and vegetables, and the luxury of good water! The incessant clatter of the Neisan is tiresome! It seems that these girls never rest, but clatter on forever. Smoke and other foreign and disagreeable odors fill my room, and add to my discomfort. I am alone. The guide always leaves me in the evening, that I may write or make out plans for the following day, which we carry out or change, as circumstances may decide. Any one starting for the interior of Japan, and expecting to find the least approximation to the food or comforts of his beloved home, will be grievously disappointed.

FROM BANGE TO SENDAI.

Definition of a "gentleman"—School children—The freshet—Crossing the Okawa—Carrying bundles—Wakamatsu—Japanese doorways—More shrines—Takinozawa Pass and Mountain—Kutsukake—Lake Inawashiro—More rain—Yamagata—The anti-express—Nakayama Pass—Freshets again—Motomiya—Curious people—Japanese and American customs.

We leave Bange this morning at 9.15, with no prospect of a clear day for our journey to Lake Inawashiro.

Before leaving the inn, an officer from the police station calls to say that the chief of the police does not understand the term "gentleman," given him as my occupation in America.

When a traveler arrives at any of the inns throughout Japan, he is immediately waited upon by an officer, who asks for his passport, of whose contents a careful record is made before it is returned to him.

The word "gentleman" does not correspond with the Japanese idea of a profession. The officer tells me that any one who does right is surely a "gentleman," but that the term does not explain my occupation. He must have my trade or business for record. I try to explain to the guide the use of the word in our country, and tell him that I am one of those unfortunates who hold government bonds and other securities, paying only two or three per cent., instead of six, and that my occupation at present is to cut off the interest coupons from month to month. Both guide and officer are puzzled over this business of "bond clipper," as in Japan a man is generally an officer, rice-grower, blacksmith, boatman, farmer, artist, carpenter, or has some similar occupation. The officer requests us to call upon his chief, and satisfy him upon this point, so getting into our jinrikishas, we proceed to the chief's office. I do not get out, and the guide who represents me without doubt has a "hot time," for when he comes out his face is red. But he laughs and says it is all right. I do not know what he has told the chief, but am convinced that "bond clipping" has been entered upon the Japanese records as a new profession.

While the guide is absent I am much interested in watching the drill of some sixty or seventy school-children, about six or seven years of age. The school-house is a substantial square stone building, standing a hundred feet from the main road. The teacher, a pretty young Japanese girl, is leading them with songs; whether sacred or national airs, I cannot say. They sound to my ears more like a Zulu war-cry.

The march is accomplished with good effect. Before entering the school-house the ranks are broken, and the children run pell mell to a large trough of water, where they slip off their wooden shoes and wash their feet, then form into line and march with songs into the schoolroom, as do our children at home. The sight is a very pretty one, and I am glad to see modern ways taught these little ones, who will some day assist in the improvements that Japan sadly needs in her social and business circles.

Before we go very far we see evidences of the freshet. Field after field is inundated, and in many cases the rice is floating upon the surface of the water. Hundreds of men and women are at work straightening up the drooping heads and trying to save their crops from total destruction. Had the freshet occurred ten days ago the rice in this section would have been ruined. Now the berry is well matured, and it is not injured by the drenching.

The road in many places is covered with two or three feet of water, through which our men wade. As we proceed we find that the Okawa is subsiding, but when we reach its banks we perceive that there will be great difficulty in crossing, and that it will be impossible to take our men and jinrikishas with us. There are many natives traveling, and our chances for securing wagons on the other side is very slim indeed.

Taking a couple of coolies to carry our baggage, and removing our shoes and stockings and rolling up our trousers, we walk over a bridge, constructed as before, of planks loosely placed on sampans which are held together by a strong iron cable stretched from bank to bank. In the centre of the river, a half-dozen of the sampans having been washed away in the night, we enter a boat, and two men, holding fast to the cable, pull us across the intervening space. The river is high and the current swift and strong. We cross over safely to within a hundred feet of the opposite bank, when, there not being boats enough to finish the bridge, we wade to shore in water nearly up to our waists.

The men suggest carrying me, but I say no, I will wade with the rest, and jumping in do the best I can. Sharp stones in the river bed cut my feet so that several times I am near falling, which affords great amusement to the spectators on the bank. Reaching terra firma we secure the only disengaged jinrikishas in the place to take us to Wakamatsu. We wish two more for our baggage, and it is suggested that a runner be sent to the nearest village, two miles off, for these; but he has scarcely started when to our joy two wagons come up, and are immediately pounced upon by my guide. Now all is well again, and we are off after many obstacles and delays.

While we were resting at the last tea house I observed a number of middle-aged women, scantily clad, also resting and sipping their tea, with great bundles lying at their feet. I was so much interested in them and their bundles that I requested the guide to ask one of them the weight of her burden and how far she had carried it. I learned that the bundle weighed forty-five pounds, and she had walked fifteen miles with it; also that this weight and distance are of small account, as many women carry burdens of from two hundred to two hundred and fifty pounds on long journeys.

The country here is flat and monotonous. Its only attractive features are the mountains seen in the distance. These are O-Bandai and Ko-Bandai, the latter, six thousand feet high, was an active volcano in 1888, destroying many villages and more than four hundred and fifty inhabitants. Rice is the chief product in this section. Here we see the industrious farmer working in his fields in his large mushroom-shaped straw hat, with a straw mat thrown over his shoulders to protect them from the sun.

We arrive at Wakamatsu in time for lunch, and ride to a very handsome inn, the Shimizu-ya, in which we find first-class accommodations. The little tea girls are pretty, clean, and attractive, with smiling faces and pearly teeth.

The day is only partly clear. Great clouds now and then obscure the rays of the sun and render the atmosphere pleasant; but when the sun does appear and shine upon the moist air and vegetation the temperature is that of a hothouse. These fumes of heat, which are common to the summer season of Japan, are said to be the source of much of the sickness of the country.

I am continually reminded of the small size of the natives, for all their doorways are made for men of their own stature, and I am constantly bumping my head as I enter the inns, as I never remember this important fact until too late. After a good and bounteous lunch of rice, fish, eggs, and tea and a restful nap, we leave, somewhat reluctantly, this delightful place, and at 2.15 P. M. say farewell to Wakamatsu, with a prospect of fair weather to the end of the day's journey. All through the country on either side of the road are many unostentatious shrines and images of Buddha. Some of these stone shrines have no torii, others have one and often two placed before the sacred emblems. Small stone images, supposed to represent Buddha, are conspicuous upon the roadside. We not unfrequently see the devout natives kneeling before them in silent prayer. The group called Koshin, carved in wood or stone, is a common sight on the sides of the roads throughout the country.

So uncertain is the weather in Japan that clouds have gathered heavily about us, and notwithstanding our hopes and fair prospects we are again in the midst of rain. But the tourist must be prepared for a drenching at any time. The country is prettier after leaving Wakamatsu, and the many natives that we meet on the way attract and interest us. Volumes might be written about these charming, odd, and happy people.

Takinozawa Mountain and Pass are before us. The road here is very rough, composed apparently of ruts and rocks. Although but recently made the heavy rains have made travel hard in many places. We have three men to each wagon, and yet it is with great difficulty that we reach the top of the mountain. We are frequently obliged to walk considerable distances in consequence of bad breaks in the road.

We are now more than seven hundred feet above the level of the sea, and have a beautiful view of Wakamatsu, with its twenty thousand inhabitants, and the country for miles around. Although it is raining fast we halt here to feast our eyes upon this exquisite picture of plain and mountain. Having descended by the Takinozawa Pass we climb by the Kutsukaka Pass to the top of the mountain of the same name. Kutsu means horseshoe, and kaka hanging mountain. From this height we have another magnificent view of the lofty peaks, O-Bandai san among the rest. O means great, and Bandai is the name of the province.

We soon reach the village of Tonokuchi, and stop at the Ingarishi inn. The inns in these districts are generally small and the accommodations limited, and it is not uncommon for eight or ten men and women to be lodged in one room, in size about ten feet square. As there are no beds these people will huddle together, and never think of complaining of their quarters.

Since leaving Bange this morning we have made but nineteen miles, owing to delays and the rough roads of the mountain passes.

To-morrow we must rise at five o'clock, to take the six o'clock steamer for an hour's ride on the beautiful Lake Inawashiro.

I awake at five o'clock to hear the rain still beating on the roof of the inn. This is a great disappointment, as during the past few days my camera has been useless in consequence of the bad weather; and I determine not to start out in the rain as neither clothing nor shoes will dry in this damp atmosphere. At all the inns and cottages they cook by charcoal fires placed in pits, so there is no hope save in the sun.

Before breakfast I have a hot bath in an immaculate tub, in water almost at boiling point. The young girl who attends me comes in and asks in pantomime if there is anything she can bring me. I assure her that I have all that I need, and she withdraws. This hot bath is a great comfort, counteracting, as it does, the chilling effects of this damp weather. We have a good Japanese breakfast, served by several Neisans with willing hands and smiling faces.

The rain subsides in time for us to take the nine o'clock steamer, so, gathering our things together and packing our wet clothes, we say good-bye to the landlady and her little maids. When one leaves an inn, especially a foreigner, it is customary for the landlady and her entire household to come to the door and bid him farewell, with a cordial invitation to return.

The small steamer is not much more than a tub, and really seems unsafe for passengers upon such a body of water; however, as adventure seems to be in the very atmosphere we breathe, we shut our eyes to the danger, and trust in Providence to see us safely through. A shrill whistle announces the time for departure, and we leave the village of Tonokuchi without excitement or commotion of any kind. We take a diagonal course across the lake to the village of Yamagata, a distance of about eight miles.

This lake is a picturesque body of water, nearly square in shape and probably ten miles each way. It is surrounded by mountains. We can distinguish O-Bandai and Ko-Bandai from the steamer's deck. The water is roughened by the rain and wind, and our little tub rides much as an eggshell on the ocean. So much spray flies over us that, at the captain's invitation, my guide and I seek shelter in his cabin.

I am told that large quantities of fish are caught in these waters. We expected, on arriving at Yamagata, to take jinrikishas and proceed directly to Motomiya, a distance of seven ri, or eighteen miles, but we learn that there are no jinrikishas in the place. This is a dilemma. I ask the guide if there is no "runner" who can engage wagons from the neighboring village? He replies that there are no wagons in any of the villages near by.

While we are considering the situation, I espy a very old and dilapidated wagon, springless, and with seats of strong, uncovered boards. "What is this?" I inquire. "Perhaps we can hire it, if there are horses or anything to draw it." We learn that this is the "regular" stage coach, Heaven save the mark! which runs between Yamagata and Motomiya, and are only too glad to find anything running between these towns that will save us the long hard tramp with our own legs. We engage two seats and room for our baggage in this unattractive vehicle. We are the only passengers. I wonder if those who have ridden in this coach have died from the effects of "anti-express."

We start in an hour, but the delay does not concern us, for we are not in condition to foot it. While waiting, I wonder what kind of horses will be attached to this rickety affair, but say to myself, "Rest thy soul in peace. All will be shown thee in good time." At the end of an hour the steeds appear. I can hardly believe my eyes. These poor, crippled, lank, and lifeless creatures! At first I laugh and then I sigh; then I am angry at such cruelty to horses. But, alas! I am not in the "States," and cannot hand the poor animals over to our society to be shot and turned into buttons, gloves, etc. The ancient harness has seen much rain, and become green with mold, as the only washings that horses, harness, or wagon ever receive are from the clouds above. Well, we must make up our minds either to go by this stage or walk with our heavy baggage. Of the two evils we choose the least, as we suppose, and set out by the coach.

I anticipate a great shaking up in this cumbersome, springless old wagon, with the roads in the wretched condition left by the recent storms, and groan to think of nearly eighteen miles of misery. We start, not swiftly, but step by step, at a gait so slow that at times it requires close attention to know whether we are going or standing still. Then at a sudden lurch over a rock or down a hollow, how we bounce about! My head strikes the top of the wagon many times, and I fall back into the seat or into the lap of my guide, wondering if the next time I am to take a "header" through the torn curtains or out by the door.

We keep up such a constant laughter that our driver, a young lad dressed in a coat and hat, thinking something is the matter, asks the guide what is wrong, apparently unconscious of our mishaps, and considering the turnout up to date, and quite the proper thing. At one dreadful rut I really am thrown through the door. Now, with slow but sure steps, we are wending our way through the Nakayama Pass, which is very picturesque, with trees along its mountain walls. The ascent is one ri, and the descent two ri, or about five miles. Going down, at a soft and bad part of the road, where the mountain is steep, whether from a caprice of the horses, or the driver getting his lines entangled, this antediluvian rig very nearly topples over the precipice. The danger is such that the guide and I leap from the coach.

When the horses are stopped the stage stands on the extreme edge of the rock, at an angle of some forty-five degrees. It is no joke, I can assure you! We right the wagon and go on.

It now begins to rain, and the air grows disagreeably chilly.

The roads in this section are the worst one can imagine. It would be impossible for a jinrikisha to travel over this one. We continue to pitch and bounce until I have a severe headache, besides pains in other regions. I must hold on tightly to prevent myself from being thrown from the wagon.

The country is unattractive, save in the villages through which we pass, where something of interest is always to be seen.

Again we are in danger of being thrown into a ravine ; this time thirty feet deep, and a second time the guide and I jump out. The driver, however, is quite unconcerned, and with a smile, a jerk, and a nod, clambers back to his seat, and we go on peacefully, though roughly.

At last, by the grace of heaven, we arrive, full of pains and aches, at Motomiya Station in time to take the 2.57 P. M. train to Sendai, having been four hours and one-half coming eighteen miles. At the station we learn that the bridges are washed away, and the railroad damaged as far as Aomori ; also, that no southern trains from Tokyo had arrived at this station since the night before last, as the bridges on that section of the road are also unsafe. A pleasant state of affairs, truly ! And my northern trip to Aomori and Yezo in jeopardy.

Rain has been falling in northern Japan since the twenty-first of July, and the largest freshet ever known in this district is engaging the attention of the inhabitants, especially farmers and railroad men. People of all trades are greatly alarmed at the present conditions.

This is the topic of conversation everywhere. The wagon roads are also impassable farther north, and it is feared that there is heavy loss in the destruction of rice crops and property in general.

While I am waiting for the train, the people gather about me in large numbers, gazing intently in my face and watching every movement, until this kind of a free exhibition becomes too much for me, and I request the station master, through my guide, to allow me to enter the enclosure, hoping there to escape the curious throng. But even here I am not free from their inquisitive stares. They stretch their necks, and some of them climb on the fence, smiling at my oddities, or standing spellbound at the strange sight. What a relief to see the train approaching to relieve me from my very annoying position. We take second-class tickets to Sendai. The third-class compartments are crowded with natives, and the comforts are limited, besides the freedom of the costumes is not pleasant to one who has enjoyed the American system of traveling. There are no conveniences on the third-class cars, while many of the second-class cars have toilet rooms.

Traveling through Japan one sees rice growing everywhere, especially in the northern central districts. Of course there are other products, but it is rare to find anything in large quantities except the mulberry. There is little to attract the eye along this line. The country is monotonous. As we approach Fukushima we see on our left Azumasan, which was the scene of an eruption four years ago. We pass small bridges that have been swept from their places by the recent freshet. Roads and fields are in many places completely submerged. There are two long tunnels between Motomiya and Sendai. Bits of pretty scenery occasionally appear, but taking it altogether the journey is tedious.

In lack of something better I fill in the time by enumerating the customs of Japan, which are in direct contrast to ours in America. Among these are the following:

AMERICA.	JAPAN.
We eat with knives and forks.	They with chopsticks.
We eat soup first.	They last.
We write with pen and ink.	They with brush and paint.
Our people are addicted to kissing.	In Japan they never kiss.
Our houses are tall.	Theirs are of one and two stories.
We have smoking cars.	They smoke in all their cars.
Our women are generally young at forty.	Theirs are old at twenty-five.
Our babies are carried in the arms.	Theirs upon the back.
Our men smoke large pipes.	There, men and women smoke small pipes.
We use small theatre tickets of pasteboard.	They large wooden tickets.
We wear hats.	They go hatless.
We wear leather shoes which touch the ground.	They wooden shoes raised some four inches from the ground.
Our purchases are wrapped in paper with the name of the firm outside.	They invariably have the name of the firm inside.
We pass vehicles and persons on the right.	They on the left.
We eat fish cooked.	They generally eat it raw.

We wear shoes indoors.	They either go barefooted, or wear a covering called a "tabi."
We shake hands upon meeting or parting with friends.	They only bow.
Our clothing generally fits closely.	Theirs loosely.
We wear jewelry.	They wear none.
Our trees are tall.	Theirs are small.
We use handkerchiefs made of linen.	Theirs are made of paper.
We use coal for heating, etc.	They burn wood.
Our writing-paper is somewhat square.	Theirs very long and narrow.
We frequently ride in carriages.	They mostly walk.
Our sleeping rooms are dark.	Theirs are lighted by lanterns.
We drink tea from large cups.	They from small ones.
We sit upon chairs.	They upon the floor.
Our rooms are elaborately furnished.	Theirs are bare and unfurnished.
Our carpenters plane from them.	Theirs towards themselves.
We sleep on beds raised from the floor.	They sleep on mattresses upon the floor.
We write from left to right.	They from right to left.
We write across the page.	They up and down.
The front of our book is the back of theirs.	
We use horses.	They men.

Many more such comparisons could be made, but these are sufficient to give an idea of the strange manners and customs of the people in this far-off country. The ladies of Japan dress elaborately and with expensive decorations of silk and gold embroideries, but these exquisite pieces of needlework are never exposed to public view. They are all on the inside of the garments. When the dress is taken off and hung up this beautiful lining is visible, but at no other time. The outside of the dresses are plain and of inexpensive material. This is another noteworthy contrast to the fashion in America, as well as in most civilized countries.

I have seen a number of these profusely decorated and costly garments, whose wonderful embroideries are completely concealed from the eyes of the world.

Flies, mosquitoes, and fleas are the only things that seem to be common to both countries, and to have the same manner of carrying on their unpopular mission.

It is hardly necessary to say that Japanese shoes are unlike ours. Many different shapes and kinds are worn. The most common are the Cata, made of wood; the Zori, made of plaited straw, and the Waraji, plaited of common straw and tied over the ankle by strings of straw.

The railroad tracks in Japan are generally three and one-half feet from rail to rail.

FLOOD AND FRESHET.

Sendai—An American room—A terrible night—Bridges swept away—We abandon the northern trip—Yaita—Rivers still rising—Impassable roads—A long, wet walk—Jinrikishas at last—Crowded inns—A hopeless prospect—Disease among the natives—Crossing the Kinugawa—In the Rapids—Coolie-back—The Furussata—Ravages of the storm—Holding the train—En route for Nikko.

WE reach Sendai at half-past seven this evening, having traveled to-day by steamboat, stage, train, and jinrikisha, and I can assure you we are tired and sore, especially so from the hard usage of the stage. We go directly to the Matsu Hotel, a European (Japanese) hotel, from which may the fates preserve me in the future! I ask the landlord to show me an "American" or "European" room. I would like some of these architects who plan European or American rooms in Japanese inns supposed to possess all the comforts of a modern home, to have one glance into a genuine American or European apartment. They seem to think, also, that if a room has a bed with four legs, regardless of springs or blankets, that it is in modern style, and with two frail and rickety chairs and a candle in a candlestick upon the table, you have all the comforts of a Western home. In this room there are no carpets, curtains, or shades; no paper on the wall, and no furniture save that which I have mentioned. It is so unpleasant and unhomelike that I tell the innkeeper to take me to a Japanese apartment, where I feel more comfortable, because my surroundings are in keeping with the country and its people. My night experience here is a terrible one. The rain comes down in torrents, and with such violence that I cannot sleep. The wind blows furiously, and at three o'clock the house shakes so that I fear that nothing less than an earthquake or a tidal wave has come upon us.

I rise and dress, and as I sit upon the floor with a lighted cigar in my hand I make up my mind that if I am spared through the night I will bid farewell to Sendai early in the morning. The storm does not abate its violence until half-past seven in the morning. It is still raining, however, and the oldest inhabitants here declare, as those in other places, that in all their lives they have never known such violent and long-continued storms, and it is impossible to doubt their statements.

Bridge after bridge is reported as washed away by the swollen waters of the rivers and lakes, and we learn that we cannot proceed farther north, for the railroad bridges and the road itself are so badly damaged that it is impossible for trains to pass north from this point; also that the bridges south of us have been swept away and the railroads badly damaged. Thus our retreat from this place seems to be cut off north and south. There have been no trains from Tokyo to Sendai since last Wednesday. The telegraph wires are broken, and communication has ceased all over the island. I learn, however, that a local train will leave here at ten o'clock, and proceed as far south as possible.

In company with many anxious natives we bid farewell to Sendai and step on board the train. This means that we have abandoned the northern route. It is a sad disappointment! But there would be weeks of delay while the railroad company is repairing its tracks and bridges, and travel might still be uncertain in consequence of continued storms. Our progress is slow on account of the serious condition of the tracks. The rivers we pass are much swollen, and small creeks have increased in size until they seem like rivers. At every station we observe great uneasiness and alarm, and although it is still raining, anxious groups may be seen everywhere, discussing the dangers that threaten them. I am much troubled, but try to make the best of the situation, and the guide and I cheer each other by recounting our experiences over bridgeless torrents and through rough mountain passes.

I learn this morning that the Kitakami-gawa, only a short distance from Sendai, has risen eighteen feet and six inches in the past two days. The fields and portions of the wagon roads are inundated, and in some of the villages through which we pass the first floors of the cottages are submerged, compelling the inhabitants to seek other quarters, in many cases provided by the police officials. There are no indications of clearing weather. The Kinugawa has risen twenty feet, the Akaborigawa, seventeen feet, and most of the other rivers are fully fourteen feet above their normal tide-mark.

We reach Yaita at ten o'clock in the evening, having been twelve hours on the road. Here we learn that our train can go no farther, as the tracks have been washed away in many places, and to add to our anxiety, it is announced that the heavy iron railroad bridge crossing the Kinugawa has fallen at one end. This is the last straw. A delay of a few days during temporary repairs could be borne, but this break will require weeks of labor ere the bridge can be fit for travel.

We try to secure jinrikishas to take us to the river, hoping to cross by sampans before it is too late. No wagons are available, as there are only five in the place, and they were engaged yesterday. Our only course is to walk to Furuta Station, a distance of thirteen Japanese miles. Japanese distances are generally reckoned as in Ireland: so many miles and a bit; the "bit" may be any length, from one mile to twenty.

It is doubtful whether we can cross the river. A heavy steel cable has been stretched over it, and to this boats are fastened for foot-passengers, but the latest reports are that cable and boats are likely to separate at any minute, as the river is a raging torrent.

We go to the nearest inn, and I retire to bed, trusting in a kind Providence to help us out. It is eleven o'clock, and the rain is beating on the roof. My guide knocks on the screen door, and says that he has hired four coolies to carry our baggage in the morning, but that we will be obliged to walk. The highway from Yaita to Nagakubo is in many places wholly submerged, so we will have the pleasure of not only walking, but wading through water waist-high.

It is a time of great excitement! The only things I fear are tidal waves and earthquakes. I pass a wakeful and anxious night. The many days of exposure to the elements, combined with fatigue, have resulted in a bad cold and a sore throat. I doctor the guide and myself as well as I can.

We rise at five in the morning to hear the latest reports on the condition of river, road, and railway. Yes, we must walk. No wagons can be hired at any price. The few horses, used for farming purposes, have all been secured to carry people to Nagakubo. I envelop myself in my waterproof, with an oiled canvas wrapped about my legs, and raising my umbrella to protect myself as far as may be from the violence of the rain, step out upon the flooded highway. We have not gone far before I am thoroughly drenched, as my umbrella is of no use whatever, and my waterproof leaks badly. The water is very high, but I am thankful we are not compelled to swim. We walk along the railroad for many miles, and where the bridges have been washed away we cross by boat, or wade to the opposite side. It is a tedious, disagreeable journey. Wet to the skin, and chilled to the bones, I wonder when the hardships of this trip will cease.

On we go, passing many natives, men, women and children, all walking except a few women who have been fortunate enough to secure horses. Two or three women are on one horse, riding man fashion and without a saddle. They present an odd picture, and were it not for the rain I would like to stop and photograph some of the scenes along the way. After a long wearisome journey we reach the village of Nagakubo. Here we endeavor to secure jinrikishas to take us to Ujii, four miles distant, but none are to be had, so we direct our coolies to go ahead with the baggage and engage rooms for the guide and myself at the inn in the village, and if possible to send us two jinrikishas. We wait patiently for more than an hour, during which time I am surrounded by about sixty natives who watch every movement, and laugh heartily if I yawn or sneeze. I light my pipe, then write down some notes, they watching with the greatest interest. Only one who has passed through such an ordeal can understand my feelings at thus being the centre of a crowd of curious men, women, and children. I tell the guide we had better walk on, although we have several parcels and are fatigued with the long tramp in our heavy wet clothing. The rain still comes in bucketfuls. The crowd opens to let us pass, and as I look back I see them still standing in the road gazing after me.

We have not gone more than a mile when we see two jinrikisha men with empty wagons running towards us. Thank Providence! They are sent by our coolies. We jump in and enjoy a much-needed rest. The men are obliged to walk in consequence of the condition of the roads, thus we make but slow progress, with such violent jolting that if we do not hold on tightly we are in great danger of being pitched out into the mud. In the course of time we arrive at Ujii, where we find only second-rate accommodations, but are grateful for any shelter at all. The inns in all these villages are filled to overflowing with native pilgrims and other travelers. At Yaita, where we slept last night, the inn was so full that as many as eight men and women were packed together in small rooms, nine feet by ten in size. This is repeated in this hotel. The police stations throughout the district are also providing accommodations for the wayfarers. At times it is difficult to obtain even inferior rooms. As we are wet and chilly I administer a full dose of quinine and saké to the guide and myself.

Our first business, before changing our wet clothing, is to ascertain the prospect of crossing the Kinugawa to-night. Our landlord says the railroad bridge is in such a weakened condition that not even foot-passengers are allowed to go over it, and that the temporary bridge of boats was washed away this morning.

I am not satisfied with this hopeless report, and request the guide to go to the police station and obtain authentic information. He confirms the landlord's statement.

Still unwilling to give up hope, I suggest that we cross the river in a boat, with a cable stretched over both ends, and pulled by men stationed on the banks. But I am told that last night a man was so determined to cross this raging flood that he attempted it with a single boat and some oarsmen. No sooner did the boat strike the rapids than it was carried swiftly down the current, threatening every moment to capsize; finally it turned over, and its occupants were given up as drowned. However, they were found this morning, down the river, three miles from where they started, saved only by a miracle. The river rose six feet last night.

Since every plan fails, I resign myself to remaining here over-night, hoping to make an early start to-morrow, and try to cross the river at a point five miles from here, and if we succeed, to take jinrikishas and ride fifteen miles to Utsu-No-Miya, where we can take the train for Nikko. While I am writing, the guide comes to say that another break is reported in the railroad between Utsu-No-Miya and Nikko. However, I can cross but one bridge of trouble at once, and the latter emergency will find its corresponding action.

The rain has ceased, the wind is blowing, and heavily laden clouds are hastening across the sky.

The first thing a Japanese does after making arrangements to stay at an inn over-night is to remove his heavy clothing, and put on a light kimono, with a silken sash. I also invariably follow this custom when traveling in this country. Tea is brought to my room, and with a cigarette, I am happy and comfortable, shutting out for a time the troubles which perplex me.

I have seen much disease in Japan. This country is noted for the cleanliness of its people, but with all their washing they are unable to cleanse themselves from this inheritance. In out-of-the-way places, where clothing is scant, the half-naked bodies of the natives reveal sores and ill-health. In the cities this is not so evident, as more clothing is worn than in the country towns and villages. I carry my own drinking-cup, and wash from a good-sized basin that has been scoured until it shines like gold. We are up at five in the morning, and learn that the prospect for crossing the Kinugawa in large sampans is favorable.

My guide secured three jinrikishas last night, and at 6.15 this morning they are at the door. While waiting for the guide I am stared at by a large crowd. One young woman, looking at me from her doorway, is absolutely naked, and I also stare at her in wonder. We each, no doubt, think what a queer creature the other is. As we leave the village the sun peeps through the clouds, and the air is like that of a spring morning. I dare not think how long this will last, for heavy clouds are even now grouping themselves on the horizon.

The road from Ujii to the Kinugawa is in good order, and our men run the entire distance of five miles without stopping. In Japan a foot measures four inches more than our standard feet, consequently their miles are longer in proportion.

In a short time we reach the river bank, where we find assembled fully a hundred natives, men, women, and children, who also are waiting to cross. Among these is a Japanese officer of high rank, who served in the Japanese-Chinese war. We make his acquaintance, and he formally presents to me his card, upon which I hand him mine. Much pleasant conversation follows, with the guide as interpreter. His card bears the following name and title: "S. Lamejima, Le Colonel, Chef d'Etat, Major de la Garde Imperial." He wishes me success in my journey through Japan, and regrets that I have had such unpleasant experiences during the past few weeks.

The efforts of my guide to have the three jinrikishas and their men carried over the river in the large sampan cause considerable delay. The owners of the boat declare that it will capsize with such a weight, and that it would be a dangerous experiment to attempt it. However, after much bargaining and persuasive arguments, the wagons, men, baggage, and ourselves are snugly settled in the bottom of the boat.

The river is wild and angry and the current swift. Strong men steer the boat with long bamboo poles as we shoot out into the rapids. How we twist and turn! Sometimes it seems that we must surely capsize and everything be lost, but these strong armed men, with nerve and skill, keep the boat steadfast to its course. The excitement is at its height when we are in the middle of the stream, where the current is deepest and the waters form a whirlpool, foaming and threatening to engulf us as they rush madly over us, drenching us to the skin. After a severe struggle, lasting nearly a half-hour, we reach the other side, and find our boat aground in three feet of water.

Our next experience is being carried "pick-a-pack" by coolies to dry land, which is a sort of an island. Our wagons and baggage are also brought to shore in safety.

We walk about a quarter of a mile over mud and stones till we come to a swollen stream, the Furussata, generally a small and unpretentious current, now a rapid river enlarged by the recent rains. We cross it by another large boat. While waiting on the bank I perceive, not far away, the wreck of the large railroad bridge which spanned this water only a short time ago. In ten minutes we are safely landed, though over shoe-tops in mud. The river has subsided six or eight feet since yesterday, otherwise we would be unable to cross it to-day. There has been great loss of life and property at this point. Dozens of cottages have been swept away by the flood in the last few days. Only yesterday a house in the neighborhood was washed away, and the whole family of five persons drowned. The inhabitants say that this river has not been so swollen for sixty years. We walk half a mile on solid ground, then resume our jinrikishas, bid the courteous Japanese officer farewell, and start off on a six-mile ride to Utsu-No-Miya Station, arriving at 10.10 A. M., just as the bell rings for the train to start for Nikko. My guide unselfishly begs me to enter the train and go on to Nikko, while he will await the arrival of the jinrikisha with our baggage and follow on the 12.30 train. But I tell him I will not desert him at the last minute; we will both wait. He urges me repeatedly, and finding me persistent in my refusal asks the guard if he cannot hold the train a few minutes till the men appear. The obliging guard consents to wait ten minutes, saying that beyond that he dare not delay the train.

The greatest interest is manifested by all the railroad officials in the arrival of our jinrikisha. Some of the passengers, wondering what is wrong, get out and ask questions. A crowd quickly gathers at the station and around me. Minutes pass and no sign of the jinrikisha. Finally, when it is within two minutes of starting time the men and wagon are seen in the distance. A shout of joy goes up, and a half-dozen men from the station run at the top of their speed to meet the tardy jinrikisha, and all together fairly make it fly to the station. It is exactly twenty minutes past ten when the baggage is placed on board the train. Another glad shout fills the air. I bow and smile and try to thank the people for their good-will, and they bow and bow, and now we are steaming along in comfortable cars to Nikko. I think often of this incident, as well as of many other kindnesses shown to us by these good-natured people, and wonder would an American train wait a traveler's convenience in any State in our Union?

In Japan I can honestly say that whether we ask courtesies of the railroad or police officers, innkeepers or jinrikisha men, we have been treated with a uniform kindness that is worthy of note. We arrive safely after a short journey, and reach the Nikko Hotel in time for a late tiffin. Few events of importance have transpired during our absence. The little stream, the Daiya-gawa, near the hotel, has become a wild torrent, whose pitching and tossing makes a noise like that of a miniature Niagara. The main wagon road bordering the stream is so washed in places that it is impossible to reach the hotel by jinrikisha. Great landslides are visible on the mountain sides, and cascades have found their way into the hollows, and fallen trees and exposed stumps suggest that a battle has been fought hereabout. And truly there has—a fierce battle of the elements. I am informed that a half a dozen or more persons have been drowned in this neighborhood in the floods of the past few days.

TOKYO AND A CIRCULAR TOUR.

We leave Nikko—Nakada—Tokyo by night—Novel sights—A fencing school—Asakusa Park—Shiba Temple—Cherry banks of Koganei—Master wrestler—Carrying a god—Tokaido—Valley of the Sakawagawa—Gotemba—Fuji-yama—Image of Kwannon—Nagoya—Shinachu Hotel—Many merchants—Great earthquake of 1891—Husking rice boats—Cormorant fishing—Ibuki-yama—Lake Biwa—Vestiges of the storm.

AFTER a rest of a couple of days we take up our regular plan of travel, proposing to leave here to-morrow for Tokyo. It has been raining in Nikko for the past five days, and is still raining. We learn that the railroad between Nikko and Tokyo is badly washed, and in some places covered with water to a depth of ten or twelve feet, and that passengers to the latter city are conveyed by boat over the breaks in the road and across the rice fields to places of safety; also that we can go to Tokyo in ten hours, three of which are by boat. A boat capsized this morning and its occupants were thrown out, but none of them were drowned. We are hoping for more favorable reports, but will, in any case, attempt to reach Tokyo to-morrow by the early train. There are many other visitors in Nikko and the neighborhood who are also anxious to be in Tokyo to-morrow, and will take the train with us.

We rise early and find the sun shining brightly, as if to give us a good send-off. We leave Nikko by the 7.30 train. The country around the city, seen upon a clear day, is charming. The lofty mountains are covered with verdure, and the Daiya-gawa, in all her moods, is picturesque. We arrive at Utsu-No-Miya Station, where we change cars, and in about twenty minutes take another train, which carries us to the village of Nakada. We can go no farther by train, for although the water is subsiding in other places the tracks here are under three or four feet. Large sampans await us, and taking our places in one of these, with other passengers, we are sculled to a temporary station provided by the railroad company.

We have been rowing over a submerged village, where the houses are under twenty feet of water. The temporary station is made of canvas stretched over long poles to protect us from the sun. Benches are here, made of rough boards. There are fully four hundred people here awaiting the arrival of the train. Having brought a lunch from the hotel we now do it ample justice. The native travelers also eat their meal of rice and tea.

We have waited here since 11.45 this morning, and it is two o'clock before a shrill whistle announces the approaching train, and an engine draws a long line of empty passenger coaches up beside the station. Then follows a comical sight! There is a great scramble for the cars. Some of the people, in their eagerness actually jump through the windows. How I would like to photograph the picture! And now they are all in and we are off, really off, for Tokyo. We cross the Tone-gawa on a fine iron bridge, which was, several days ago, under thirteen feet of water.

We reach Tokyo without further event, and go to the Imperial Hotel. In the evening we take jinrikishas and ride about the city. It is a beautiful sight; more like a dream city than one in real life. The odd-looking buildings, with hundreds of lighted lanterns hanging before them, and the throngs of pedestrians on the sidewalks are all so unlike anything we see at home, that we are filled with delight at every turn. In the midst of our enjoyment a sudden and severe shower compels us to make a hasty retreat to our hotel.

We are up bright and early this morning, eat our breakfast, and are ready for the jinrikishas which our guide engaged for us last night. We go at a good pace, for we have two strong men to each of our wagons. We go first to Kudan Park, where we visit the temple of Shokonsha, also the museum, which is filled with interesting trophies of the late war with China. We then ride to Ueno Park. This is a very pretty place, with enormous artificial lakes, rockeries, cascades, and shrubbery, and it is famous for its temples, tombs, and cherry trees.

We have a very good lunch at the Foreign Hotel, the only one in this section and the first one of the kind built in Tokyo. We then visit the Zoological Gardens close by, where we see the usual elephants, lions,

THE CONTESTANTS ARE SEATED IN A SMALL ROOM TEN FEET SQUARE.

tigers, monkeys, etc. The gardens are attractive but the number of animals is small.

Having expressed a desire to see some good Japanese fencing, our guide surprises us by announcing that he has made arrangements for a special " bout " in one of the best fencing schools in Tokyo. This news gives us great pleasure, and we soon find ourselves in the presence of the first master of this art in the city. The contestants are seated in a small room about ten feet square, waiting to be called to the arena. This arena is a space twenty feet by forty, with rough seats facing it and an awning overhead to protect us

A MAN AND A WOMAN FENCE WITH SWORDS.

from the sun. Here we are entertained for an hour and a half. Japanese fencing is quite different from that taught in the Italian or French schools.

Their manner of handling the sword is, however, dexterous, and would be effective in warfare. A man and a woman fence with swords, the honor of victory being won by the latter. Then a man with "pick and sling" competes with one with a sword, and vanquishes him.

After all the exercises are over I am invited to enter the ring and show master and pupils how fencing is taught in America. They seem surprised at the difference, and the master tries his skill against mine to the amusement of the spectators. The nimbleness and adroitness with which the Japanese fence is worthy of note. They are so quick and subtle.

The following day we visit Aasakusa Park. The grounds of this park are very large, and hundreds of natives are strolling about within the enclosure. We learn that this is one of the festival days, but even on ordinary occasions this is one of the liveliest places in Tokyo. Here may be seen rare shows, penny gaffs, performing monkeys, cheap photographers, street artists, theatrical and other figures in painted wood or clay, and venders of toys and lollipops of all sorts. Here also are the Pagoda and the great bell tower, in which the bell, which is heard all over the city, is rung at intervals. The interior of Aasakusa Temple is well worth a visit. This temple is dedicated to Kwannon, and a fabulous antiquity is claimed for the image worshiped here which, it is said, was drawn up in a fishing net on the neighboring coast by an exiled nobleman in the early part of the sixth century. The wonderful image is never seen, but it is supposed to be only an inch and three-quarters in height. The disproportion between the size of the image and the vastness of the temple has occasioned much remark.

The temples of Shiba are among the chief marvels of Japanese art, especially the highly ornamented gate

INTERIOR OF AASAKUSA TEMPLE.

called Ni-ten-Mon and the magnificent tomb of the second Shōgun, which would repay any one who has time to study them closely. Wonderful is the amount of labor bestowed upon the temples which are seen everywhere throughout Japan, and well may it be called the country of temples. Volumes could be written

Shiba Temple Gate, called Ni-ten-mon.

upon the traditions, architecture, carving, and surroundings of these masterpieces of art, and even then the subject would not be exhausted. In the Murray *Handbook of Japan* may be found many traditional and historic records of the sacred edifices.

It is late in the season for the Cherry banks of Koganei, and there are only green leaves on the trees that form an avenue two miles and a half in length along the canal, but we can imagine the beautiful sight about the middle of April with the gay crowds assembled under the pink and white blossoms. Now scores of natives are promenading along the banks of this little stream. The thoroughfare is so crowded that we are obliged to leave our wagons and walk. It is really a great sight, this gathering of men, women, and children of all ranks and conditions.

As we return to the city we visit the school of Nobu Shige Tago, Master Art Wrestler. Here in a room twelve feet square is given a private exhibition of wrestling by boys from ten to sixteen years of age. The professor is a good teacher, judging by the skill of his pupils. These boys are taught to become professional wrestlers. On our way back to the hotel we pass along the quays and by some dismal streets to the main thoroughfare.

Tokyo is a vast city, and contains nearly a million inhabitants. This afternoon we have a fine opportunity of seeing the various tradesmen at work in their shops. While passing through one of the side streets we have a curious experience. We suddenly come upon a crowd of many hundred people of both sexes and all ages, huddling together, screaming, and apparently fighting over a small temple borne on the

WHILE PASSING THROUGH ONE OF THE STREETS WE HAVE A CURIOUS EXPERIENCE.

shoulders and thrown from side to side in the struggle. As the crowd comes our way I am somewhat alarmed. Not wishing to be in the midst of a mob, I call the guide, and ask him what it means? He tells us to get out of the wagons and stand aside until the frantic throng has passed. It seems that the natives frequently carry a small temple on their shoulders through the streets. The temple is supposed to contain a god, or rather the spirit of one, and if allowed to stop before a house the inhabitants of such house will be haunted by a demon. Consequently, all the people before whose houses the temple passes make every effort to prevent its stopping. Hence the dreadful scrabble, some of the people insisting that it shall stop, others madly determined that it shall move on.

At last we reach our spacious and elegant hotel, which is upon the European plan. The table is good, and meals are served in courses. How much could be written of Tokyo! But much would always be left unsaid, for Japan is interesting at every turn, whether in city or country.

We leave Tokyo for Yokohama to-day at 1.30 P. M., and arrive in two hours, going to the Grand Hotel, where we rest and plan a circular tour to Kyoto, Osaka, and Kobe, which we hope to accomplish in two or three weeks.

At 8.30 this morning we leave Yokohama, expecting to reach Nagoya at half-past seven this evening, and go on to Kyoto to-morrow. The railroad in many places runs parallel with the old Tokaido, or highway between Tokyo and Kyoto, and from our car windows we see many jinrikishas and pedestrians on this road. The word Tokaido signifies "Eastern sea road," and was given to the road at an early date on account of its running along the seashore in an easterly direction from Kyoto, which, being the old historic capital, was regarded as the starting point. And even at the present time it seems as if all roads lead to Kyoto.

FROM OUR CAR WINDOWS WE SEE MANY PEDESTRIANS ON THIS ROAD.

From the seventeenth century onward the Tokaido was traversed twice yearly by Daimyos coming with gorgeous retinues to pay their respects to the Shōgun at Yedo, and all the chief towns here, as well as on the other great highways of the empire, were provided with especially fine tea houses for their lordships' entertainment. The greater portion of the beautiful avenue of pine trees which lined this road still exists, and may be seen from the car windows. The railroad on which we are traveling was begun in 1872, and completed in 1889. It reduces to seventeen hours the journey from Tokyo to Kyoto, formerly laboriously accomplished on foot in twelve or thirteen days. The day is charming, the air clear and cool. We are fortunate enough to have a first-class compartment to ourselves, and can make ourselves perfectly comfortable.

After we leave Fuji-sawa the beautiful mountains of Hakone come into view, and many fine bits of scenery are visible from our car window. Now on the left the ocean spreads itself out to add a greater charm to the picture. At Kozu our road turns inland to avoid the Hakone Mountains. Here the country is wild and rugged. Now and then we see a queer looking little house of one story with a roof thatched with straw. The scenery is impressive, with an abundance of picturesque subjects that I shall not soon forget. At Yamakita we have an extra engine attached to carry us up an ascent of fifteen hundred feet to Gotemba Station, which is the highest point on this line. The mountains here are so numerous that we pass through tunnel after tunnel in rapid succession. I counted seven of them within a short time.

At Sano we have a magnificent view of Fuji-yama in

all the glory of its majestic height, standing out against a cloudless sky, and presenting one of the grandest landscapes in the whole of Japan. This giant mountain, the pride of every Japanese, can never be seen to greater advantage than to-day, as it rarely appears so perfectly free from clouds to its very summit. There

FUJI-YAMA IN ALL THE GLORY OF ITS MAJESTIC HEIGHT.

are many other lofty mountains quite close to our beloved Fuji. It is a scene of wonderful beauty, almost too great for words. We gaze and gaze until it vanishes in the distance. I sit silent, thinking of the noble mountain, of the towering peak in its misty purple robe, heightened in color by the pale blue of the sky at its back. The surrounding mountains too are blended in such perfect harmony of color! Yes, this is the greatest scene in Japan.

Glimpses of the ocean and distant mountains come to us as the train winds serpent-like upon its course. When we stop at the stations the natives, as usual, stare, and call their friends to look at us.

Between the stations of Washizu and Toyohashi the guide-books tell you that a fine bronze image of Kwannon, ten feet high, dating from the year 1765, can be seen perched on a pinnacle of rock. We strain our eyes to see this relic, and at last perceive it, but it is so small that one could easily pass by in the train without noticing it.

Between Yokohama and Nagoya we cross several long and well-constructed iron bridges, spanning wide rivers. The trains do not slacken their speed while going over them or in passing through the tunnels, and I think of the probability of accidents and our poor chances of escape in some of these narrow passes. After twelve hours of continuous travel we reach Nagoya at 8.30 P. M., and ride at once to the Shinachu, a foreign hotel. While at supper we are surrounded by merchants, who offer various wares for sale. They all talk at once, making a perfect bedlam. Swords, wood and straw work, and cloisonné are spread out before us. These men have a peculiar habit of attacking the stranger as soon as he arrives.

We find the town full of life and interest. Its population is one hundred and thirty thousand, and it is noted for its manufacture of porcelain, cloisonné, fans, and silks. As I write I can hear from an adjoining room the peculiar native drawl called singing, accompanied by the samisen, played by some young girls. I have been in Japan long enough for these sounds to be quite familiar.

We visit the odd stores and stroll about this flourishing provincial city. The castle, now closed to visitors, is still one of the wonders of Japan. It was built in 1610 by twenty great feudal lords, to serve as the residence of Ieyasu's son. It is preserved by the imperial household department as a monument of historic interest. The golden dolphins on the top of the five-storied donjon can be seen glittering all over the city. The Buddhist temple of Higashi Hongwanji is a wonderful structure, whose exterior and interior are equally grand.

We leave Nagoya at 7.20 on a bright, beautiful morning, and part also with the picturesque Tokaido, on our way to Kusatsu. The country presents only a succession of rice plantations as far as the eye can see. Boys and girls are loitering along the road with their schoolbags at their sides, and full of harmless pranks, quite amusing to the spectator. The thrifty farmer, in his straw hat, is weeding or otherwise attending to his various fields with strangely shaped hoe and plough. Here is a group of workmen who appear like a bunch of mushrooms as they stoop over their tasks.

Natives pass along with their long poles balanced at either end by baskets containing various goods. Others carry loads no less heavy on their heads. Always interesting, the types of life to be seen on the public road are many and quaint. Off in the distance are the mountains dividing the provinces of Owari and Mino from those of Omi and Ise. We are entering the district of the great earthquake of October, 1891. At Ichinomiya most of the houses have been rebuilt and other damages repaired. The crowds of people walking hither and thither surprise us.

The houses in the villages, the shrines and temples never lose their interest for us. These shrines and temples are profusely decorated with flags and offerings in celebration of the various festivals that are held upon certain days throughout the year in the different provinces. In many of the cottage windows appear plants and flowers, offerings to the moon, which is full and brilliant at this time. As we cross the Kisogawa, which is lovely at every point, we observe a number of strange looking boats on the river, and learn that they are called "Husking Rice boats," and that their great water-wheels are turned by the force of the current.

Picturesque villages nestle at the foot of the mountains, making an unusually attractive scene, while scores of sampans move up and down, or across the stream, with huge cargoes and a single oarsman. On the mountain sides deep gulches, caused by landslides resulting from the earthquake, are visible. As we approach Gifu Station we perceive the devastation caused by the recent floods. Hundreds of acres of farm land are still under water, and men are at work upon the railroad, which was a short time since submerged.

At Gifu the famous cormorant fishing is carried on in the summer months. Cormorants are raised by the natives, and large quantities of fish are caught in this manner in the Nagara-gawa. The only point of attraction here is the mountain chain which we are approaching, and which opens to let our train pass through a narrow but exceedingly pretty valley. We have two engines now and are gradually ascending. On our right, and towering far above the others, is the great Ibukiyama, king of all the mountains in this region, four thousand three hundred feet high, and bare of trees or other vegetation, but famous in the early ages for its wealth of medicinal plants. It is one of the "Seven High Mountains" of central Japan. At Nagaoka we have a fine view of this mountain, which stands out in bold relief with its many precipices and hollows distinctly outlined in the clear atmosphere. It is a magnificent spectacle. From Nagaoka we descend rapidly, coming into a full view of the mountains that border Lake Biwa on the north and south, but no portion of the lake is yet visible. On our right, after we have left Nagaoka miles behind us, Ibukiyama looms up again with a funnel-shaped cloud now about its summit that gives it the appearance of an active volcano. The coloring of the whole picture is exquisite.

At Maibara we have our first glimpse of Lake Biwa. This beautiful body of water, really the Lake of Omi, is generally called Biwa on account of a fancied resemblance in shape to a Chinese guitar. It lies three hundred and thirty-three feet above sea level, and is thirty-six miles long and twelve wide. According to a legend long believed in by the Japanese, Lake Biwa was produced by an earthquake in the year 286 B. C., while Mount Fuji rose up from the plain of Suruga at the same time.

Everywhere around us are traces of the recent flood. Houses and shops are under four and five feet of water, and judging by marks quite plain, the water has been at least three feet higher. Small boats filled with people are being rowed from house to house and along the streets. Many of the houses have tumbled down, others are leaning and ready to fall. The railroad tracks have been repaired, but for miles the farm lands are entirely submerged. The country appears like a great lake, and the scene is one of general devastation. In consequence of this inundation we leave train at Hikone, and take jinrikishas to a neighboring inn for tiffin. The tracks are completely submerged from Hikone to Baba Station, and trains can proceed no farther.

At eleven o'clock our guide informs us that the steamboat company will run a special steamer to accommodate the great number of passengers awaiting transportation, and we hastily gather our things together and engage jinrikishas to take us to the water's edge, which is now in the centre of the town. Here we hire a large sampan, and are rowed down the street between houses that are deserted and flooded with from eight to ten feet of water. Our hearts are filled with sympathy for the poor villagers thus made homeless and penniless; yet every one we meet seems cheerful and happy. This is the natural disposition of the Japanese, no matter how great the trouble.

After rowing for a half-hour we reach Lake Biwa, and espy in the distance the little steamer that is to take us to Otsu. Hundreds of passengers have gathered at this point, and as sampan after sampan arrives with its human freight we have a picture of national life, rarely seen even by the traveler in Japan.

THE CAPITAL OF FORMER DAYS.

A steamer on Lake Biwa—Kyoto—Shops—Queer combinations—The Daibutsu—Great bells of Japan—Punishing children—Burning the body—Advertisements of medicines—Servants of the gods—Supplicating the gods—Selling children—Tsumiya, Naka-gawa-Tokumon—Kiyomizu Temple—Junk trees—Tea culture—Kinkakuji—Chion-in—The 33,333 images of Kwannon—Temple of Inari.

WE wait and wait, but there is no movement to take us on board. It is now nearly four o'clock, and the steamer was to start at half-past eleven or twelve. The traveler in Japan soon acquires the bad habit of never starting on schedule time. After being exposed to the hot rays of the sun for a long time I direct our guide to have our boat rowed to the side of the steamer and request them to take us on board. There are fully four hundred people waiting. I wonder how this little boat can hold them all! Its capacity seems about two hundred. They come and come, and the decks sink lower and lower, till they almost touch the water. And we are to travel twenty miles with this heavy cargo! Heaven help us: in case of an accident! We are packed like sardines, with no life preservers, and only one lifeboat six feet long. We are truly "between the devil and the deep sea."

However, we arrive safely at Otsu at eight o'clock in the evening, and are transferred from the steamer to land by sampans. This town also has been inundated, and temporary paths are made of wood. Taking jinrikishas to Kyoto we arrive at the Yaami Hotel, tired and hungry, and after enjoying a good supper we retire

WE STEP ON THE BALCONY OUTSIDE OUR ROOM AND HAVE OUR FIRST VIEW OF KYOTO.

to a comfortable room with clean beds, and close our eyes with prayers of thanksgiving that we have been carried safely through the perils of the day. Refreshed by a restful night we step on the balcony outside our room and have our first view of Kyoto. What a charm each new city has to our unaccustomed eyes! The whole appearance resembles nothing that we have ever seen. Instead of the tall buildings of our American cities we see houses that are very low, and only a faint white curl of smoke will occasionally appear above a roof.

Kyoto is a city of two hundred and fifty thousand

WE VISIT THE VARIOUS MANUFACTURING ESTABLISHMENTS.

inhabitants, and is famous for its pottery and porcelain, its fine embroideries, its velvets and brocades, its bronzes and its cloisonnés; also for its many temples, for there are at least a hundred and fifty of no mean size in the city. We spend much of our time riding about the city and visiting the various manufacturing establishments and the most noted temples. We are greatly entertained by the English signs that hang before some of the shops. One reads, "Milk and Gentlemen's Hats;" another, "Portrait Painter and Manila Cigars," and there are many more combinations just as odd.

Much might be said of these temples, both ancient and modern, but I shall not attempt any description, but, with a few illustrations, will endeavor to give some idea of their grandeur, architectural style, and exquisite coloring.

One of our first visits is to the Daibutsu, or Great Buddha. This idol consists only of a head and shoulders, but even thus, it reaches to the ceiling of the lofty hall in which it is kept. It is made of wood, and the head is gilded. It is fifty-eight feet high and forty-three feet across the shoulders.

In a separate building, not far from the Great Buddha, hangs one of the great bells of Japan. This bell is of bronze, nine inches thick, nearly fourteen feet high and nine feet in diameter. It weighs more than sixty-three tons, and is larger than that of Ta-chung-szu in Pekin, which has been considered the largest suspended bell in the world. Its companion in size is at Chion-in, also in Kyoto. For a few sen, given to the attendant, one may have the privilege of swinging a great log that is suspended beside the bell, which, swaying to and fro with much force, strikes the bell, producing a voluminous musical sound which is heard all over the city. The pleasure of hearing these full, rich tones is so great that I repeat the operation many times.

While traveling in Japan one is constantly and unpleasantly compelled to notice the deep scars that disfigure the bodies of the men, women, and children, as well as the numerous sores exposed to view.

Burning the body is practiced throughout Japan for three different purposes. First, as a punishment; secondly, by jinrikisha men, wrestlers, and laborers to produce strength where muscles are deficient; and thirdly, as a cure for different kinds of disease. There are special doctors in the cities and in some of the country towns who make this their profession. Learning from the guide that there are several of these specialists in Kyoto, I visit one of the most prominent of these men.

We find the doctor in his office and operating room. We sit upon the floor, and the guide states the object of our call. On the wall is a life-sized drawing of the human figure, inscribed with certain lines and dots, used to designate the corresponding places to be burned on the patient's body in cases of certain diseases or deficient muscle. On the floor in the middle of the room are two large iron pots filled with ashes upon which several sticks of red-hot charcoal rest. The day being rainy, the doctor regrets that no patients are present, but says he will illustrate the process of burning upon his own person. Suiting the action to the word he takes from a box beside him a small piece of sponge or punk, which he forms into a little pyramid, and places upon his bare arm. He lights the pyramid with a stick of charcoal, and it burns slowly until it reaches the flesh. The odor of burning flesh is quite perceptible; the pyramid is allowed to remain on the arm until a deep hole is burned. This is the whole process. Places of sometimes an inch in diameter are burned in extreme cases. If a jinrikisha man, whose work requires muscle, lacks this in his legs or arms, he is burned on the part which is deficient, and expects thus to attain the necessary strength of muscle, or, if a patient is afflicted with disease, as rheumatism for instance, he is burned on the part of the body indicated by the diagram on the wall.

As we ride through the city streets we are much diverted by the odd advertisements upon the porches of some of the shops. A burned turtle of great size, also a burned cat, dog or snake appear in separate and conspicuous spots, indicating that medicine made from the powder of such animals and reptiles is sold within. Such medicines are extensively used throughout Japan. Think of taking cat, dog or snake powder for headache or dyspepsia! These, with a thousand other things, remind us constantly that we are many, many miles away from our own civilized homes.

About the various temples are ever seen throngs of pilgrims carrying baskets of rice and other food to feed the servants of the gods, who are supposed to dwell in little wooden buildings made especially for them upon

GION STREET, KYOTO.

the temple grounds. A hole is cut in the side of the house only large enough to admit the hand. Rice, beans, and other food can be bought at the shops which line the neighboring streets. This food is thrown into the houses of the sacred servants, and the devotee claps his hands, and kneeling with bowed head prays for the blessing he desires from this especial god. Quite a thriving business is done by the shops which sell the goods approved by the gods. Thus the gods keep the people, and the people keep the gods. Here are a mother and her pretty daughter making supplications to a god; and to insure the granting of their petition

QUITE A THRIVING BUSINESS IS DONE BY THE SHOPS.

it is necessary for them to walk a hundred times around this small house. The older woman holds in her hand two hundred long narrow strips of paper, and each time they complete the circuit of the building she turns down two of the slips, one for her daughter and one for herself.

We visit some renowned cloisonné manufacturers, and observe their interesting but tedious process, which requires skill and training of the highest order. We see also the workers in Damatium, or gold and silver inlaid on steel. At my request the proprietor of one of these places presents me with a beautiful sample of the work just before completion, and still mounted on the workman's block.

In all these factories we are amazed to see such difficult work accomplished by small boys, some of them not over eight or ten years of age. We learn that it is still the custom in Japan for parents to sell their children to the tradesmen, receiving an annual income for their services; and they sell not only the present generation, but frequently children yet unborn.

Our guide arranges for a visit to "The Enclosure" and to its most fashionable inn, in which the demi-monde of the highest class dwell. The name of the inn is Tsumiya, Nakagawa-Tokumon, and we are informed that the officers of the Mikado are frequent guests here. The landlady allows us to go over the whole house. The rooms contain no furniture whatever, but are decorated with gorgeous and exquisitely embossed panels and embroidered draperies. They are named the "Fan Room," the "Peacock Room," the "Horse Room," etc., from the paintings with which walls and ceilings are lavishly adorned.

We are entertained in a large, handsome reception room on the first floor, where we seat ourselves on cushions and are served with tea and candy. Then the landlady says we may have the privilege of seeing three women of the highest rank, who are the favorites of the royal household. One by one these distinguished beauties appear in richest robes and costly jewels. They dance gracefully before us, every movement betokening delicacy and refinement. These girls are treated with the greatest honor, and are surrounded with every luxury. They neither toil nor spin, yet their glory and privileges are equal to any women in Japan. They are attended when they choose to walk about the Enclosure, and when they go into the city, which is seldom, their escort is of the highest rank. Their children, if girls, are reared to fill positions similar to the mothers. We spend an hour in this celebrated domicile, then, with an "Arigato" to our hostess, depart, much wiser than we came in matters of this kind.

I must not omit the Kyomizu-dera (dera or tera, Buddhist for temple), whose origin, the guide-book tells us, is lost in the mists of ancient fable. There is an interesting legend of the goddess Kwannon having appeared to the novice, Enchin, disguised as an old man, and bidding him build the temple, or rather an image of the compassionate one (Kwannon), of a log that lay before him. After twenty years of great difficulty

THE CAPITAL OF FORMER DAYS. 325

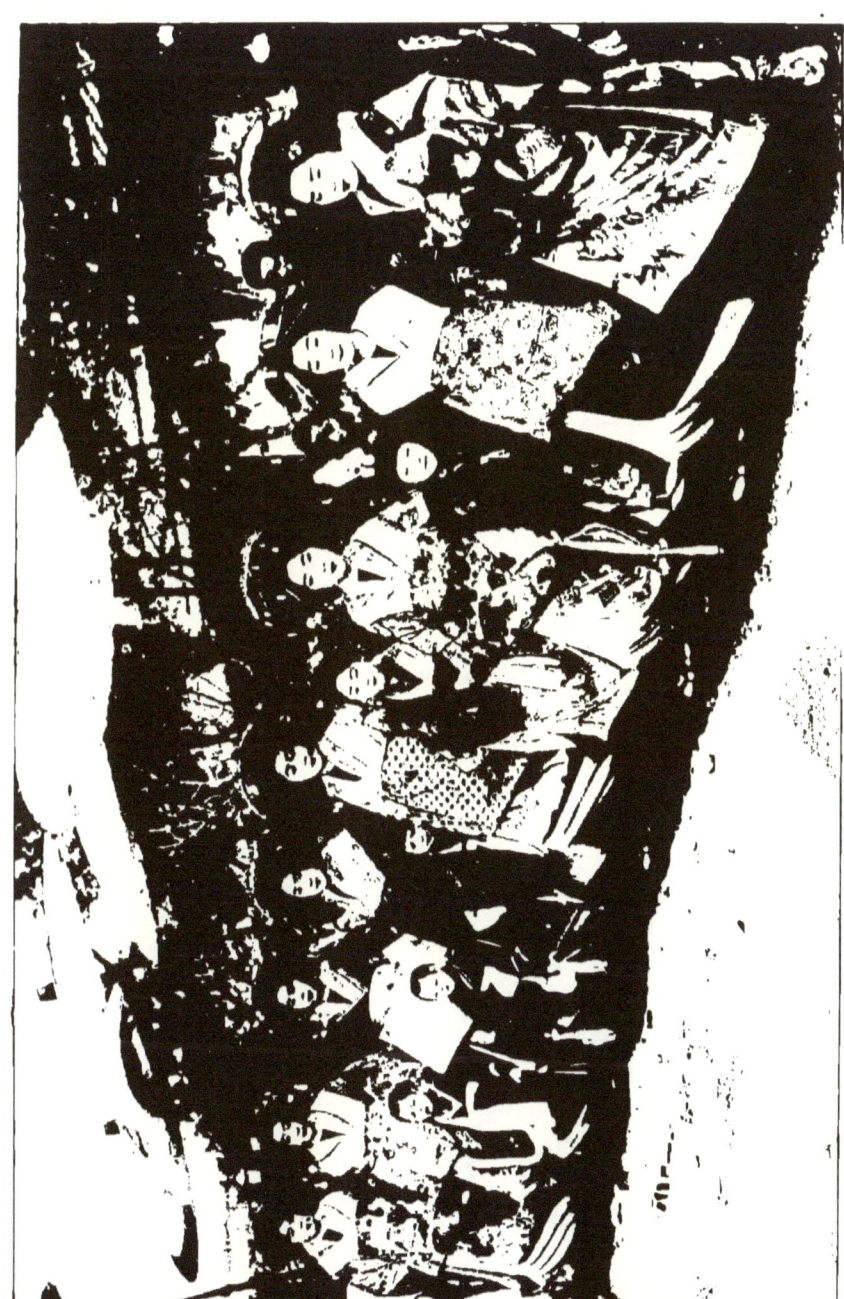

They Neither Toil nor Spin, yet Their Glory and Privileges are Equal to any Woman in Japan.

the work was accomplished, and the warrior, Sakanoe-no-Tamura Maro, chancing upon this spot in pursuit of a stag, was so struck with the untiring devotion of the

A DISTINGUISHED BEAUTY.

novice that he gave his own house to be pulled down and re-erected beside this cascade as a temple for the image.

We proceed on foot along the road named Kiyomizu, in honor of the temple. Hundreds of shops line the street, and here may be found almost any article one could name in the china, glass, or pottery line. Here are many curiously shaped and decorated cups, plates, and vases, and for a few sen the dealer will part with any article that meets your fancy.

The temple is an odd, ancient-looking structure, built

KYOMIZU DERA, WHOSE ORIGIN IS LOST IN THE MISTS OF ANCIENT FABLE.

upon massive piles. Within are many things that interest us, and we meet scores of sight-seers, as well as pilgrims and other worshipers, at the shrine of the sacred image. Walls, pillars, ceilings, and every other available spot are lavishly adorned with paintings by the old Japanese masters.

The main temple is dedicated to the "eleven-faced, thousand-handed Kwannon," whose image, a little over five feet high, is enclosed in a shrine that is opened only once in thirty-three years. Lights are always kept burning in the temple, and worshipers pass in and out all night long.

Junk Trees are Cared for, Wooden Hoops Sometimes Encircling the Branches.

In our drives we note the artistic manner in which the Junk trees are cared for, wooden hoops sometimes encircling the branches, which are also trained to represent enormous vines. The bamboo groves are also a novel sight. These branchless trees, straight as arrows, shoot up to a height of forty or fifty feet, and some of them have considerable circumference. Innumerable articles may be made of this wood.

I have scarcely mentioned one of the greatest indus-

BAMBOO GROVES ARE ALSO A NOVEL SIGHT.

tries of Japan—the tea culture. Thousands of acres are devoted to this branch of trade. The tea is generally gathered by little girls, who are quite expert in plucking the leaves. When gathered it is baled and shipped to a factory, where it is dried by artificial heat, then repacked and sent to all parts of the world. The common tea in Japan ranges in price from twenty-five to fifty sen a pound, while the finer grades command from one to seven yen a pound.

THE TEA IS GENERALLY GATHERED BY LITTLE GIRLS.

We enjoy much a visit to Kinkakuji, or more properly, Rokuonji, a monastery of the Zen sect, which receives its popular name from the kinkaku or golden pavilion in the grounds attached to it. In 1397 Ashikaga Yoshimitsu having resigned the title of Shōgun to his youthful son, built himself a palace at this place.

He shaved his head and assumed the garb of a Buddhist monk, while still in reality directing the affairs of state. The garden is picturesque, with a charming lake in the centre, bordered with pine trees, and a little pine grove island. The lake is stocked with carp, which are accustomed to being fed by visitors, and will come in crowds at the clapping of hands to where the pieces of cake or cracker are thrown. These fish are looked upon as sacred, and are never caught or killed.

The "golden pavilion," which once shone with dazzling glory, is dull and worn, bereft of all its gold. The apartments contain folding and sliding screens, and kakemonos by the most celebrated Japanese artists, besides relics and autographs of the Shōguns and other celebrities.

The temple of Chion-in stands upon a hill in eastern Kyoto. A broad avenue lined with cherry trees leads up to it. This temple was founded in 1211 A. D., by Enko-Daishi, who developed a new doctrine, called the road to the "Pure Land," from which a sect, known as Jodo, meaning pure land, was named. Chion-in is the principal monastery of this sect. These temples are universally simple and imposing, impressing one with the solemnity of his surroundings, and, like all the others, this one contains many objects of interest within its walls. Near it stands the bell tower, completed in 1618, containing the great bell. The height of this bell is ten feet eight inches, its diameter is nine feet, it is nine and one-half inches thick, and weighs nearly seventy-four tons. This bell was cast in 1633.

I must not omit the San ju-sen-gen-do, or the temple of the thirty-three thousand three hundred and thirty-three images of Kwannon. Few temples in Japan are more interesting. Here are rows upon rows of gilded images, all representing the eleven faced, thousand-handed goddess of mercy. There are, however, but one thousand large images, the number being obtained by including the small effigies on the foreheads, on the halos, and in the hands of the larger images. There are thirty-three spaces between the pillars, which form a single row from end to end of the temple.

We visit also the Shinto temple of Inari, which was founded in 711 A. D., when the Goddess of Rice, according to fable, first manifested herself on the hill behind the temple. Kobo Deishi, it is said, met an old man carrying a sheaf of rice on his back, and recognized in him the deity of this temple, hence the name Inari, which signifies rice man.

The chief entrance to the temple is by the great red torii on the main road, then up a flight of steps and through a large gate flanked by immense stone foxes, to the Haiden, or oratory; thence one comes to the chief chapel, the pillars of whose portals are plain, the rest of the walls and pillars being painted red or white.

Numberless shrines are attached to this temple, but we do not visit them all.

As we approach the little Oku-no-in we pass through more than four hundred small red wooden torii, placed so as to form two nearly parallel colonnades, one ascending, the other descending. These torii have a very peculiar effect, drawn thus in line, being of all sizes and states. As each bears an inscription relating to the donor, they are monuments to the deceased.

KOBE, OSAKA, AND NARA

A Geisha dance—Losses by flood—To Kobe—Nunobiki Waterfalls—Iwamoto, the bamboo worker—Osaka—Wrestling match—Satsuma—Cotton fields—A first-class compartment—Nara—Avenue of lanterns—Tame deer—Temple of Kasuga-no-Miya—Daibutsu—Naraningyo—Return to Kyoto—Sobei Kinkozan—Young ladies' school—Kyoto Castle—Imperial Palace.

QUITE gayly we enter our jinrikishas and set out for the tea house, in which, as we are informed by our guide, a first-class Geisha dance is to be held. On our way to this entertainment we pass a street called Zezeura Street, which is, we learn, monopolized by the demimonde. We see the frail young people sitting at the small windows, some of them looking miserable enough. This is a dismal street. The lamp on each house is so placed as to cast a bright light upon the inmate, and I pity the poor creatures, who seem to have no means of escaping their wretched mode of existence.

Arriving at the inn, we are ushered into a large room on the second floor, where, to our surprise, chairs are provided for us. The room is bright and attractive with candles and lanterns. The musicians, three girls, enter with their respective instruments and sit upon the floor in front of us, playing and singing Japanese airs. In about twenty minutes six little girls, looking like

Japanese dolls, appear, and seat themselves between us on the floor, and smile and smile, and look so charmingly innocent that we are completely fascinated. Soon one of them rises, and, stepping to the centre of the room, begins a graceful dance, keeping time with the music. Then another rises, and then a third takes her

The Musicians (Three Girls) Enter and Sit upon the Floor in Front of Us.

turn, and finally the three dance together. Each time the movement is of a different character.

The Japanese dances differ greatly from ours. They know nothing of waltzes, polkas, or quadrilles, but represent by their dances some ideal picture, such as the planting, growth, and death of a flower; the planting and harvesting of rice; a scene in which the lover pays his devotion to his lady, and others of a similar nature. After each dance these little tots come before us with profound bows, and seat themselves at our feet. The

THE WHOLE SIX GEISHAS GIVE US A BEAUTIFUL EXAMPLE OF THE VARIOUS STYLES OF DANCING.

whole six Geishas give us a beautiful example of the various styles of dancing.

When this part of the entertainment is over a sumptuous repast of Japanese food is set before us in Japanese fashion. It consists of rice, rice cakes, and rice candy, pickles, fruit, and saké. The dancers and musicians share the banquet with us. As these little creatures sit close beside us, for we too are now sitting upon the floor, they amuse themselves by admiring and touching the jewelry worn by the ladies and gentlemen of our party. A young actor now appears with a two-handled sword and executes many skillful movements. He also imitates the notes of a number of birds and animals, as well as different musical instruments, by means of a small piece of a leaf held in his mouth. His last act is something quite wonderful. He stands a bamboo stick about eight feet high and fully three inches in diameter upon the floor, and with a single stroke of his sword cuts it completely asunder. With this act the entertainment closes. The landlady bids us sweetly, "Kom-ban-wa," and the Geishas bow their heads to the floor and repeat, "Sayonara," until we are in our jinrikishas and have started for home.

Having seen the most interesting temples and other places of note in Kyoto we leave this city for Kobe. The recent rains have completely inundated the fields along our route, and much property has been destroyed. It is estimated that fifty million dollars would barely cover the losses in southern Japan by these floods. The rice fields here are still under from three to five feet of water. We arrive at Kobe at 6.20 P. M., after a journey of two hours and a half, and go to the Oriental Hotel, which is under Japanese management, and excellently conducted. The rooms are of good size, fully furnished, and combine the comforts of an English and American hotel. Meals are first-class, and a full brass band, composed of Japanese musicians, plays English and American airs during the hours passed in the dining-room, affording much pleasure to the foreign guests.

ORIENTAL HOTEL, KOBE.

Although to-day is Sunday, it does not interfere with one's plans for sight-seeing. Stores are open and business is transacted without any restrictions whatever. Beyond the fact that every city and village in Japan is interesting to the foreigner, there is little worthy of note in Kobe. We pass through the town on our way to the Nunobiki Waterfalls, and after a half-hour's ride leave the jinrikishas at the foot of the mountain and ascend on foot to the Men-daki, or Female Fall, which is forty-three feet high, and is surrounded by tall pine

MEN-DAKI, OR FEMALE FALL, KOBE.

trees. Near the fall is a pretty tea house with a fine view of the fall from its porch. Here are a dozen or more pretty little tea girls, all anxious to serve us.

In summer, when it is warm enough, the women bathe here perfectly naked, for this is their especial bathing ground. Farther up the mountain side is the On-daki, or Male Fall, eighty-two feet high, which is generally reserved for men and boys, although men and women bathe together at either fall. These are the Nunobiki

WE RIDE ALONG THE BUND OR QUAY.

Falls. As we ride through the streets of Kobe we stop at some of the shops and purchase several articles of odd patterns and curious workmanship. We then call upon the famous and only Iwamoto, whom we find engaged in a difficult carving on a bamboo cane. His work, very elaborate and highly finished, is generally executed on boxes, canes, and similar objects. He is said to excel all workmen in Japan in his special line of carving.

We ride along the bund or quay, where we see a small number of ships. Kobe was opened to foreign trade in 1868. When we return to the hotel for tiffin we are pleasantly surprised by meeting some friends whose acquaintance we made in Yokohama. How home-like it is to meet these new acquaintances at the various stages of our travel! They seem like friends of long standing. At 1.45 P. M. we take the train for Osaka, going, on our arrival, to the Osaka Hotel, which is a large building recently erected by a syndicate of Japanese capitalists. It is poorly furnished, barn-like and uninviting, impressing one with the idea that all the funds were exhausted in building and nothing left for furnishing. After depositing our traps in a cheerless room, we start out on a tour of sight-seeing.

Osaka contains many stores of no mean pretensions, which offer great inducements to the foreigner. We visit the noted Satsuma ware establishment of Yabu Meizan, the most prominent manufacturer in Japan, and are shown an inexhaustible stock of this exquisite porcelain, and, judging by his exorbitant prices, Yabu Meizan is certainly more than an ordinary manufacturer. Small teacups and saucers range as high as twenty and thirty yen apiece, and even more than that.

We have a glimpse of the castle, but do not go in, as our time is limited.

Learning that there is to be a wrestling match at the "Commons" this afternoon, we repair thither, and find fully two thousand spectators, mostly men, assembled under an immense canvas tent. When we enter, after

THE WRESTLERS ARE LARGE FELLOWS, OF GREAT WEIGHT AND MUSCLE.

paying a small admission fee, the wrestling is quite under way. At the most critical points in the contest, the audience give vent to their excitement by cries of "Ya! Ya! Ya!" They do not applaud with hands or feet, as the spectators in such places do in our country. The wrestlers are large fellows, of great weight and muscle, and wear only the close-fitting loin cloth. The umpire stands near, to settle the contest at the decisive moment. These matches may be seen at almost any city in Japan. Gambling and betting are indulged in, and they are attended by the lower classes of the people.

We return to the hotel, tired and hungry, to find little comfort and poor fare. We leave here to-morrow for Nara. We pass a wretched night, as the beds are lacking in feathers, hair, or husks, whichever it may be, although, from our feelings, the mattresses might be made of corncobs.

We take the ten o'clock train this morning for Nara, passing many acres of cotton fields where hundreds of men, women, and boys are at work. This section of the country is largely interested in raising cotton and manufacturing cotton fabrics. There are in the neighborhood, large mills of modern architecture worked by the latest and best foreign machinery.

The traveling native is always an object of great interest to the foreigner. Here is a prim little maiden, shy, coy, and proper, sitting gracefully on the car cushions, with her dainty feet under her. She never flirts or smiles. I speak of the Japanese maiden of the first class. The lower classes are much less refined in manners and customs.

We reach Nara at 11.50 without event. Nara was

the capital of Japan during several reigns, from 709 A. D. to 784. On our way to the temple of Kasuga-no-Miya, we pass through avenues of stone lanterns, of which it is said that no one knows the number. At various places along the road to the temple are small tea houses, at which one can buy cakes with which to feed the tame deer that follow the wagons. These deer are trained to bow several times at the word "O-hayo." (good morning) and always expect this reward. Then we ride through a long avenue of standing lanterns, many of which are, it is said, lighted every night. The temple was founded about 767 A. D., at the request of Take-Mikazuchi, who rode to Nara on a white deer in search of a new residence, then summoned three other gods to come and dwell with him there. The bright red of the different temples, and the numberless brass lanterns with which they are hung, are in strong contrast to the beautiful green of the magnificent cryptomerias which are seen everywhere between the buildings.

After strolling about the grounds for some time we return to our jinrikishas and proceed to the temple, which contains the largest Daibutsu in Japan. This image of Buddha, fifty-three feet in height, is in a sitting position, with the legs crossed and the right hand uplifted. It was cast in 749 A. D. The work is not so finely executed as that of the Daibutsu at Kamakura, but it is a wonderful image, and has experienced strange vicissitudes.

We walk about the temple grounds. In the spacious courtyard, in front of the Daibutsu, we see an ancient bronze lantern, carved in open work with Buddhist images and conventional animals. It was executed, it

WE PROCEED TO THE TEMPLE, WHICH CONTAINS THE LARGEST DAIBUTSU IN JAPAN.

is said, by a Chinese artist of the eighth century, and is not only the finest, but the earliest specimen of such work in existence.

We stop at many of the shops about here and make purchases, among which are several sword canes. The swords of these canes were made by a famous Japanese sword-maker named Saiyo-Kokaji-Munechika. We also invest in some small wooden figures, exquisitely carved and colored. These figures are called Naraningyo, and

LARGEST DAIBUTSU IN JAPAN.

are intended to represent the characters in the lyric dramas of mediæval Japanese literature, known as the "No Dances." There is little to interest us in Nara beyond the temples, the Avenue of Lanterns, the Great Bell, and the Daibutsu, and having seen these we take the train for Kyoto, passing on our journey thither nothing worthy of note except the large tea plantations for which this section is famous. The most expensive tea in Japan is raised here.

Once more we are in pleasant and comfortable apartments in the Yama Hotel in Kyoto. After breakfast our guide tells us that we have a "big day" before us, and must make an early start. Our shopping in this city must be finished to-day, as we leave to-morrow morning at seven o'clock for Shizuoka.

We visit first the world-renowned Sobei-Kinkozan, manufacturer of porcelain and cloisonné, who is most attentive to us, and takes great pains to explain and show us the entire process of the work. In return for his kindness we purchase some of his choicest articles.

We are then taken to a private dancing and music school for young ladies. We are much interested here in observing the different methods of instructing the young girls in the arts of dancing, music, and needle-work. The building is divided into many rooms, and the instruction is given by women teachers. In the first room which we enter about a dozen girls sit in front of a raised platform observing attentively one of their classmates, who is dancing under the individual instruction of the teacher. The movements are graceful and pretty, and considerable practice is necessary before the pupil can make either a private or public engagement. We enter many of the rooms. In some the girls are being taught to play on different instruments, such as the taiko, a sort of drum; the tsuzumi, the gekkin, the koto, and the samisen. These little Geishas, as they are called, are often pretty and attractive. Their happy and innocent faces would fill any house with sunshine.

A special permit, obtained from the Foreign Minister, is required for a visit to the castle. The well guarded buildings and spacious grounds are beautiful in their simplicity. Magnificent paintings, elaborately decorated screens and exquisite wood carvings in wonderful designs are in the many rooms through which we pass. A special permit for each individual is also required for the Imperial Palace. Upon entering the office each visitor's name is recorded in a massive book kept for that purpose. Name, date, residence, and occupation must be plainly written before any attention is shown the visitor by the attendants. The buildings and interior decorations are superb. Many hours might be spent admiring the skill of these masters who are represented here, each excelling all others in his own line of work.

NOTE.—The city of Kyoto pays its policemen from six to ten yen a month, requiring them to report for duty every other day. They are provided with clothing but not food.

LAST DAYS IN JAPAN.

Miyanoshita—A strange shampooer—The Fujiya Hotel—Bamboo canes and American climate—Hot springs—An American breakfast—Dogashima—Yumoto—Yokohama—Farewell to Japan—On board the "Coptic"—At sea—The 180th meridian—Died at sea—First sight of land—Cricket—Candy pull—Honolulu—800 coolies—Leaving Honolulu —Betting on the pilot—San Francisco—A snow storm—Summit Station —The Rockies—Chicago—Philadelphia.

WE take the early morning train from Kyoto for Shizuoka. The journey is but an hour, and our stay here is transient, as we leave on the 10.12 A. M. train for Miyanoshita. As we leave the station I observe the crowd staring at a calm, dignified Japanese personage attended by five officers with swords. Upon inquiry I learn that this is Mr. Kabayama, the present Home Minister of Japan, and late general in the recent Japanese-Chinese war.

The ride from Gotemba Station to Oyama lacks interest, as mist and rain obscure our view of the beautiful, majestic Fuji-yama. We arrive at Kozu at half-past twelve, and take a horse tram-car to Yumoto, which is the terminus of that line. Here we take jinrikishas and ride to Miyanoshita, arriving at the Fujiya Hotel at 5.45 P. M. What we can see of the country through the mist is wild and mountainous. It must be picturesque and beautiful when the day is clear. The rain seems as though it has come to stay, as is usually the case with rain in Japan. This hotel is conducted on the European plan, and is very elegant as well as admirably managed. The rooms are clean, spacious, and first-class in every particular.

VIEW OF TONOSAWA.

Last night I engaged a shampooer to give me massage night and morning at the rate of twenty-five sen an hour. This massage is quite different from that in our country, and much less pleasant. The man, who assumed the title of a professional, insisted upon putting his feet on the bed and rubbing me in that manner. I objected to his creeping over my bed, but he said it could be done in no other way. I then took off the sheets and told him to give me the treatment on the mattress.

This morning it is still raining, and a heavy mist hangs over everything. We had intended remaining here a few days to visit the Hakone Lake region and take the famous Ten Province Pass to Atami, but as we are informed by a guest in the hotel that the rain has been pouring for several days, and there is no prospect of clear weather, we decide to pack up and hie away to Yokohama. We manage, however, to take in some of the scenes about us. The hotel is beautifully situated, surrounded by lofty mountains whose towering peaks seem guarding us. A pretty garden is in front of it, and there are lovely walks for those who come here in dry weather. Not far from the hotel is the village of Miyanoshita, a small settlement, composed almost entirely of shops, where one may purchase trinkets and souvenirs, inlaid work, canes and fancy odds and ends for a few sen. These articles are pretty and cheap, but let the tourist beware of those made of wood, and if he thinks that the climate of Japan and America are similar, let him take the advice of those whom experience has taught otherwise. Almost every article of wood when unpacked in America is found ruined by shrinking. These articles are generally made of bamboo, which is susceptible to a change of climate. (Out of twenty canes bought of Iwamoto at Osaka, all quite expensive, only one reaches Philadelphia in a perfect condition, the others having split from top to bottom.)

We visit the hot springs here, where the men and

MIYANOSHITA ROAD, NEAR YUMOTO.

women are seen bathing together, perfectly unconscious of their nudity.

The village of Sokokura is also interesting on account of its magnificent scenery, and because there one can indulge in the pleasure and refreshment of the hot baths.

We leave Miyanoshita this morning, after a good American breakfast. At this hotel, one can obtain beefsteak, lamb chops, eggs, coffee with cream and sugar, rolls, butter, and all the delicacies of a first-class café in our own country.

The country around the hamlet of Dogashima is beautiful beyond description. Picturesque little villas nestle in the forest, and it seems that one could pass his life happily in this charming spot. Cascades, large and small, wind through the rocks on the mountain side. Along the Miyanoshita road the scene is no less fair. Can there be a region more beautiful than this?

Picturesque Japan offers to artist, poet, scholar, material for the work of a lifetime. We might truly call this part of the country a family of mountains, for mountains are seen at every turn, and so majestic and lofty that man realizes his insignificance in the presence of these masterpieces of creation. Farther on is Tonosawa. What a grand panorama is before us! We pass many of the natives, among them, pretty little maidens, quaint and effective bits of color in the landscape.

We continue on the Miyanoshita road as far as the village of Yumoto, still in the midst of scenes of magnificent beauty. The distant mountains, clad in every shade of green, blend their hues with the foliage in the foreground, producing a picture of soft atmospheric effect, that would inspire the soul of an artist. We pass an attractive little inn at Yumoto, and come to Sammai-hashi, which has nothing to distinguish it from the other villages along the road. Now the mountains are less high, and the scenery less sublime. We cross several bridges and finally arrive at Yokohama, where we are cordially received by the proprietor of the Grand Hotel, and settle down to a time of rest, varied by shopping and preparations for our voyage home. Everything earthly must have an end, and so we have come to the last days of our visit to Japan.

Saturday, October 10th.—This is the day of our departure. With packages and bundles, large and small, we look our farewell from window and porch, and, with our faithful guide, take our last jinrikisha ride to the pier, where the hotel steam launch waits to carry us to the steamer "Coptic" out in the harbor. The day is wet and disagreeable, yet many friends accompany us on the launch, and wish us bon voyage on the steamer's deck. Promptly at eleven o'clock the gong is heard, and the bell rung for visitors to leave the ship. At 11.30 we weigh anchor, a bell sounds on the bridge, the indicator bids us go ahead, and we take a last regretful glance at the mountains, valleys, and temples of Japan, as they fade forever from our sight. The cabin passengers number thirty, all pleasant, congenial people. The high winds and rain of the past few days have made the ocean rough and unpleasant, in consequence of which many of the passengers are compelled to retire to the privacy of their staterooms. The rain continues through the night and the sea becomes more turbulent, causing trunks and bundles to dance about our stateroom in a very lively manner.

At daybreak I look out of my porthole to see what the prospect is for clear weather. The waves are pitching us about with great force, but the sky is clear, and the indications are for a fair day. It is Sunday, but there is no service, as nearly every one is too sick to attend. Our life on shipboard is much the same from day to day. The passengers are by this time over their seasickness, and games and other social amusements fill the hours.

To-night we will cross the one hundred and eightieth meridian, and will then pick up the day dropped on our journey to Japan. We will retire to-night, it being Friday, and wake up to-morrow and still find it Friday, but when we leave it this time it will be a day less in life's calendar. There are eight hundred steerage passengers on board, mostly Chinamen, who are being transported to Honolulu on contract, and who will be scattered among the various islands for farming and other work. We now have the most delightful weather. The sea is smooth and the temperature pleasant.

The chief steward of the vessel died of heart disease on Friday night. He had been confined to his bed a long time, and was not personally known to the passengers. The officers of the ship endeavored to keep the fact of his death a secret, but the cabin passengers were all soon aware of it. Our steamer is like a city, where only a wall may separate the extremes of joy and sorrow. The steward was buried at sea on Saturday, the 17th, at half-past nine in the evening. How solemn was the service, and how brief! As his body sank to its last resting place I thought of the eyes that had taken their last look, the arms which had taken their last embrace, and felt a great sympathy for the heart left sorrowing and desolate.

The weather is still delightful. This morning, Sunday, October 18th, we have our first sight of land since bidding good-bye to Yokohama on the 10th of the month. The land is Birds' Island. The captain at my side assures me that we will be in Honolulu to-morrow morning by half-past nine or ten o'clock.

Have you ever heard of playing cricket on board of a steamer? Well, after leaving Japan, our enthusiastic purser made up two full teams, and we have had a match from two o'clock till four, every afternoon except Sundays. Our games are full of excitement, and we enjoy them greatly.

Last night we had a candy pull, which was a "howling success," and made much merriment, although more candy was distributed on the chairs and floor than among the passengers.

Honolulu, October 19th, 6 A. M.—Before the steamer is docked, the eight hundred coolies from Hong Kong are transferred to boats, and taken to quarantine close by. Having had breakfast on board, we procure a carriage and drive through the most beautiful streets of Honolulu, and along the picturesque road to Waikiki. We never tire of these charming scenes. Here we meet some of the friends we made during our visit here, and we greet each other with the glad and cordial welcome of old friends.

At four o'clock this same day, we are again on board the steamer, with our faces set toward San Francisco. What a scene of life and gayety is here as we embark. The Government Hawaiian Band, numbering thirty pieces, is on the pier playing patriotic airs, while a party of about twenty Kanakas sing native songs in the steamer's saloon. Our friends, as before, bring great sweet-scented "leis," and cover our necks and shoulders with the fragrant offerings. Amid shouts and cheers, music and song, and the minor tones of half-sad, half-smiling farewells, the good ship lifts anchor and bears us away.

The voyage to San Francisco is without event. The customary diversions fill the hours, and the days repeat themselves.

On Sunday, October 25th, at 1.10 P. M., we sight the Farralone Islands. At this point the temperature of the water is 50°, while the atmosphere is 60° These islands are but twenty-eight miles from the harbor of San Francisco. Now the pilot's yacht comes into sight, and as the passengers crowd forward to catch a glimpse of this important personage, the men entertain themselves by betting which foot he will place first on the steamer. There is much laughter when he leaps on deck, planting both his feet on the boards at once. All bets are declared off, amid roars of merriment.

Now the doctor and Custom House officers are received on board. It is Sunday, and we are all disappointed to learn that we can take only our hand grips on shore. Trunks and larger pieces of baggage are to await the inspection of the officers on Monday. At six o'clock we go ashore, and after mutual farewells we wend our way once more to the Palace Hotel.

Monday, October 26th.—This morning we return to the steamer and have our baggage passed, and so ends the long voyage from Yokohama to San Francisco, a distance of five thousand and fifty-eight miles. We spend three days in San Francisco, then start on Friday, the thirtieth of the month, by the Southern and Union Pacific road for Chicago, thence over the Keystone Limited to Philadelphia. After leaving Sacramento we pass through miles and miles of snow-sheds. Snow fell last night, and the ground is covered with its winter coat. The peaks and sides of the Sierra Madre loom up white and glistening. We travel comfortably in the drawing-room of our Pullman car.

Saturday.—It is 12.55 P. M., and we are approaching Humboldt Station. The wind is blowing a gale and tearing the autumn foliage from the trees. Looking across the plain we see a grand snowstorm. Dust and sand are drifting through the cars, although we are protected by double windows. Eyes and noses are sensitive to this, and we begin to sneeze.

At Winnemucca Station rain and snow are still dominant, and the air is chilly and unpleasant. We arrive at Ogden on schedule time. The snow is four or five inches deep, and it is still snowing. The Rocky Mountains gleam out white and ghostly in their fleecy robes. Since leaving Sacramento our ascent has been constant. At Summit Station we reach an altitude of seven thousand and seventeen feet, then gradually descending we come to Ogden, where the elevation is four thousand three hundred and one feet. From Ogden we again ascend to Sherman Station, the highest point on this route, eight thousand two hundred and forty-seven feet above the level of the sea. We make a gradual descent from here until we reach Chicago, which is only five hundred and ninety feet above sea level. Thus far the journey across the country has been monotonous and the scenery uninteresting. We are now passing through Echo Cañon. The long range of the Rockies does not attract one, and the only beauty in the landscape here is the crystallization of the ice and snow upon the trees and bushes. The forms are as varied as those of a kaleidoscope, and one may gaze and gaze and see ever new shapes of glistening light.

Here and there an old Conestoga is drawn up a short distance from the road, its occupants evidently enjoying a rest, and the horses unharnessed and hitched to the wagon, while through the roof projects a stovepipe, from which the smoke is curling gently heavenward. What a sea of desolation, and apparently far from civilization!

We reach Chicago Tuesday, November 3d, at 7.40 A. M., only five minutes ahead of schedule time, having traveled more than two thousand three hundred miles without changing cars. We leave Chicago at eleven o'clock and arrive in Philadelphia at 12.17 P. M. on Wednesday, November 4th, thus happily terminating a delightful journey of nearly seventeen thousand miles without accident.

www.ingramcontent.com/pod-product-compliance
Lightning Source LLC
Chambersburg PA
CBHW020242240426
43672CB00006B/613